David & Charles Locomotive Studies

THE ENGLISH ELECTRIC MAIN LINE DIESELS OF BRITISH RAIL

Brian Webb

DAVID & CHARLES
NEWTON ABBOT   LONDON
NORTH POMFRET (VT)   VANCOUVER

ISBN 0 7153 7158 4

Library of Congress Catalog Card Number
75-43206

Set in 10 on 11 English
and printed in Great Britain
by Biddles of Guildford
for David & Charles (Publishers) Limited
Brunel House Newton Abbot Devon

Published in the United States of America
by David & Charles Inc
North Pomfret Vermont 05053 USA

Published in Canada
by Douglas David & Charles Limited
1875 Welch Street North Vancouver BC

CONTENTS

David & Charles Locomotive Studies

Locomotive Monographs

General Editor:

O. S. Nock, BSc, CEng, FICE, FIMechE

INTRODUCTION AND ACKNOWLEDGEMENTS

Since the introduction of diesel-electric locomotives on British main line railways over 40 years ago, the name of English Electric has become synonymous with this form of traction. The first post-war main line units owned by the home railways were equipped by English Electric, while apart from a dozen or so, all the English Electric-built and equipped diesel-electrics built under the BR modernisation programme are still at work giving good account of themselves.

Alone among BR diesels can English Electric locomotives claim virtual freedom from serious engine troubles, and they have never had to suffer the power-deratings or re-engining of other types. Moreover, the English Electric engine has been used to re-engine other makes of locomotives in large numbers.

More English Electric diesel engines have been supplied to BR than any other make, and they are the only manufacturer to have equipped or supplied locomotives covering the whole spectrum of BR power from 350 to 3300bhp. The immediate future portends the extension of this to 3520bhp.

The success of British diesel traction overseas is also due largely to English Electric, whose design and engineering team make the work of Gresley, Stanier, Collett, and Bulleid assume proper perspective, and the success and longevity of UK-built diesel power overseas is the very bane to our much-vaunted foreign competitors.

The tenacity of the British locomotive industry to diesel-electric transmission has brought it much partisan and ill-informed abuse, but in spite of the diesel-hydraulic locomotive protagonists' assertions, we have seen this type of traction pale in little over a decade to almost insignificance and become—so far as high power traction is concerned, apart from Hungary, some communist countries, and of course Germany, its attributable country of origin, although this is debatable—virtually unsaleable. Signs show too, that even in the role of shunting the diesel-electric system is making a come-back, especially in the higher powered range.

It has been said in the light of the energy situation that the diesel locomotive is doomed to replacement by electrification. However, with only about 10 per cent of the world's railway mileage electrified by 1975, it would seem unlikely that much above 20 or 30 per cent would be achieved at the current rate of progress by the end of this century.

*   *   *

To keep this work within prescribed limits it has not been possible to include the English Electric shunting locomotives in detail nor in their entirety every aspect of the main line locomotives, but I have endeavoured to give broad coverage in a factual and informative account of this remarkable family of locomotives. Conflicting private and official information on the locomotive naming dates has presented problems, but so far as can be seen at the time of going to press the lists are accurate.

Many people have contributed invaluable assistance to the preparation of this book and the author would like to record his thanks to Norman Gardener of GEC Traction Ltd (which incorporates the English Electric Co Ltd), A. C. Baker, J. Duncan, H. C. Hughes, M. Harris, C. R. Parker, D. Kay, plus the officers and members of the Railway Correspondence & Travel Society, the Stephenson Locomotive Society, and British Railways Board.

Photographs chosen have benefited from the assistance of Ian S. Carr, who placed his entire collection at the author's disposal, GEC Traction, British Railways, Westinghouse Brake & Signal Co Ltd, K. Hoole, J. M. Boyes, N. Skinner, S. C. Nash, R. C. Riley, H. D. Bowtell. Other photographs from the publisher's collection are the work of P. J. Fowler, G. T. Heavyside, D. Cross, and C. R. L. Coles.

The manuscript was typed by Miss D. L. Scheetz, to whom I am most grateful.

Brian Webb.

And the first shall be last: No 50050, renumbered from D400, heads the 10.45 Paddington-Weston-super-Mare at Flax Bourton near Bristol on 21 June 1974. *(P. J. Fowler)*

CHAPTER 1

ENGLISH ELECTRIC

The important contribution made by The English Electric Company Ltd to British and world diesel-electric traction has never been given the accolade it warrants. This seems strange considering that the British steam locomotive, which was in use widely throughout the world, received so much attention—almost, one might say, quite disproportional to its importance—from railway historians and writers. The achievements of the modern traction side of the British locomotive industry concern a number of manufacturers, but the majority of large diesel locomotives, diesel-traction engines, and associated equipment both for export and for home use, is directly attributed to English Electric.

The English Electric Company Ltd was formed in 1918 from the merger of Dick, Kerr, and Co Ltd, Preston, and Phoenix Dynamo & Manufacturing Co Ltd, Bradford, the former having already owned Willans & Robinson Ltd of Rugby since 1916. It also purchased the works of Siemens Bros Ltd, Stafford.

Of these constituents, Dick, Kerr, had recently built and supplied 40bhp 60cm gauge petrol-electric locomotives to the War Office equipped with Phoenix generators and Dick, Kerr, axle-hung traction motors. These units may with certainty be considered as the ancestors of the BR 350/400bhp diesel-electric shunter. Siemens had supplied electric locomotives for home and overseas use, while the inclusion of Phoenix and Willans in the group gave the added bonus of electric traction equipment and heavy oil engines, respectively. From that time English Electric was mostly concerned with electric traction work and the diesel field was largely left to Armstrong Whitworth of Newcastle-upon-Tyne and Harland & Wolff of Belfast, both of which did a good range of diesel-electric units between them from 1929 to 1938.

It was indeed the former firm which built the first British main line diesel-electric shunter and main line locomotives during 1932/33, so in spite of claims made in 1947 for 10000 and 10001, they were not the first main line diesels on BR—that honour must go to Armstrong Whitworth. There was some parallel to Armstrong Whitworth and English Electric in that the success of their work was the ability to produce within their own organisations most of the traction equipment needed for their products.

Around 1910, R. & W. Hawthorn, Leslie & Co Ltd, also of Newcastle-upon-Tyne, was trying to interest railways in its proposals for main line 'thermo-electric' locomotives of up to 1000bhp. These machines were petrol-electrics designed and patented by W. P. Durtnall under his various 'Paragon' systems. (See *British Internal Combustion Locomotives 1894-1940*.) There is little doubt that while the rest of Europe was expensively wasting time on such things as diesel-direct drive, diesel-compressed air, etc, this Tyneside company, in association with Durtnall, had already decided that the future lay with electric transmissions, and that one would have been built in 1914/15 if war had not broken out, and probably tried on British main lines. During 1920 a twin-bogie twin engine thermo-electric was built, but little came of it.

The association of Hawthorn Leslie with English Electric started in the 1920s when they built a number of electric locomotive mechanical parts for the latter company for use in locomotives erected at Preston. It was not until 1933 that English Electric decided to build its first diesel-electric locomotive and the mechanical construction was again entrusted to Hawthorn Leslie; it appeared in 1934 as we shall see later.

During the remainder of that decade, a handful of shunters, including some for export to the African continent, were built under the Hawthorn Leslie-English Electric association. In 1939 Hawthorn Leslie amalgamated with Robert Stephenson & Co Ltd to become Robert Stephenson & Hawthorn Ltd (RSH), with works at Newcastle and Darlington. At the time of this link an order for three main line 450bhp 1-BB-1 diesel-electrics for the Eastern Railway of Brazil was in hand and were the first main line diesel-electric locomotives, as opposed to railcars, supplied by English Electric. In common with the shunters, these units had English Electric diesel engines and electric traction equipment.

During world war II, English Electric did not build any diesel-electric locomotives, and its first post-war main line order was not received until 1946. This contract was from Egypt for 12 1600bhp 1A-Do-A1 diesel-electric main line locomotives, being followed by one for shunters also. The main line order made use of the Dick, Kerr, works erecting shop at Preston for six units and, for the first time, the vast capacity of Vulcan Foundry Ltd (VF) at Newton-le-Willows, which built six as subcontractors, the forerunners of hundreds of English Electric diesel-electrics from that works. Subsequently, the manufacture of English Electric diesel locomotives was carried out mainly by Vulcan Foundry, and in due course ceased entirely at Preston.

The link between the Darlington and Newcastle based Robert Stephenson & Hawthorn Company and Vulcan Foundry dated back to the 1830s, but RSH and VF merged formally in 1944, while from March 1955 they both merged into English Electric (EE), the manufacture of EE diesel locomotives then being carried out at both plants.

This gave English Electric the real advantage over other British locomotive builders, for it now had within its widely flung empire the full capacity required to build locomotives virtually *ad infinitem*. Moreover it had a prime advantage in being able to produce its own engines and transmission equipment with little chance of competition from its fellow locomotive builders, especially in main line work.

In due course the VF and RSH were fully integrated into the EE Group as the Vulcan and Stephenson works. During the 1950s and early 1960s steam building ceased at these works and a decline in orders brought closure of the Forth Banks works, Newcastle, in 1960, and the Darlington Works in 1964, all locomotive construction then being concentrated at Newton-le-Willows.

The formation in 1967 of English Electric-AEI Traction arising from the merger of English Electric with Associated Electrical Industries—itself incorporating British Thompson, Houston Ltd and Metropolitan Vickers Ltd—gave the largest and probably most experienced rail traction group in the world.

An even larger grouping was soon to follow when, in 1968, GEC (General Electric Co Ltd) took over the whole of the EE-AEI group. The severe rationalisation which followed saw the virtual elimination of the manufacture of locomotive mechanical portions at Vulcan Works by 1969/70, the procedure then being to use spare capacity in other manufacturers' works, such as Metro-Cammell Ltd. GEC Traction Ltd nevertheless remains a formidable force in rail technology, and it alone of the world's rail industries can claim a direct line of descent from the Stephensons and from the first thoughts on diesel-electric traction.

left: The first English Electric diesel-electric locomotive, a 300bhp 0-6-0 DE shunting locomotive built as a prototype by Hawthorn, Leslie in 1934, HL 3816/34. *(GEC Traction Ltd)*

Right: **Fig 1:** Diagram illustrating diesel locomotive wheel arrangements: driving axles are denoted by letters—A = 1, B = 2, C = 3 etc—and non-driving axles by figures.

Below left: Superstructure frame of BR Deltic class 55 under construction at Vulcan Foundry. *(GEC Traction Ltd)*

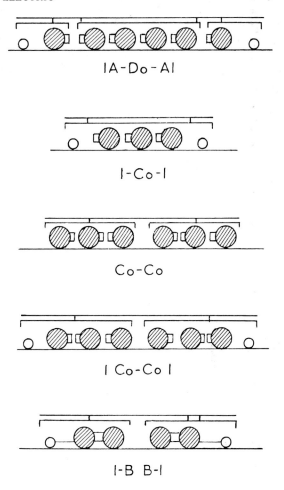

IA-Do-AI

I-Co-I

Co-Co

I Co-Co I

I-B B-I

The English Electric diesel-electric locomotives for BR operate on the established diesel-electric principle of diesel engine coupled to a generator, providing power to electric traction motors. All employ the conventional twin-bogie layout with variations in axle layout. They are either full width cab or bonnet/hood type, with slight variations in detail design, generally with superstructures built from rolled or cold formed steel sections panelled to form load bearing structures. Panelling welds are ground flush to obtain an exterior smooth finish. Deck plates are continuous to prevent oil and water leakages, suitable drains and collecting areas being provided. Light alloys and glassfibre is used, where suitable, for doors, hatches, ducting, tread-plates, tanks, etc. Bogie designs vary to suit axle layout, weight restrictions, adhesive weight and service requirements. A complex routine test programme was evolved by EE to ensure that all parts of each locomotive were tested before leaving the works.

The role of the diesel-electric shunter

At this point it is pertinent to consider briefly the place of the 350/400bhp 0-6-0 diesel-electric shunting locomotives supplied for use on the British main line railways over the past 40 years in the general line of diesel development.

The success of this machine saw it gradually replace steam shunters from the second world war and although in the 1950s and 1960s it was assisted in this by a large fleet of lower-powered units with mechanical or hydraulic transmissions, the latter types have mostly been withdrawn.

Of a total of 1382 350/400bhp 0-6-0 diesel-electric (DE) shunters, only 173 had makes of engine other than the English Electric 6KT type, and these too were withdrawn often after relatively short lives. Another feature of the 1209 EE-equipped shunters is that all but 11 were built in the railways' own workshops—the 11 being the LMS and GWR units of 1935/6 built by R. & W. Hawthorn Leslie/English Electric.

The SR at Ashford initiated the practice of building mechanical parts for 0-6-0DE in 1937, followed in 1939 by the LMS at Derby with the only non-standard batch of EE-equipped shunters. This batch was based entirely on 10 Armstrong-Whitworth units built for the LMS in 1935/6, and perpetuated that maker's equipment layout, but using EE equipment. They had a single frame-mounted traction motor driving through a jackshaft to the wheels; 40 were built, 10 of which went to the War Department (WD) for military railways.

The final derivative of the 1934 prototype was first put in production during 1944 at both the LMS Derby works and the LNER Doncaster works. They used two axle-hung nose-suspended traction motors, outside frames and the familiar fly-cranks and side-rods which typify the type, with EE traction equipment.

Above: Superstructure frame of a class 40 locomotive under construction at Vulcan Foundry. The class 37 had a similar superstructure design. *(GEC Traction Ltd)*

Below: The English Electric type 12CSVT engine and associated generator being lowered into the partly finished superstructure of a class 37 at Vulcan Foundry. *(GEC Traction Ltd)*

The first 14 Derby examples went to the WD, but following construction was for the LMS. At nationalisation in 1948 a total of 51 0-6-0DE with EE equipment were taken over by BR, with others under construction.

Other workshops were soon building their own regional versions of the 1944 Derby design, Swindon in 1948, followed by Ashford in 1949 and Darlington in 1952, the latter building the Derby design without alteration. With the introduction of the BR standard 0-6-0DE in 1952 a massive programme was put in hand involving Darlington, Derby, Crewe, Horwich, and Doncaster works, which jointly produced no fewer than 1193 units by 1962; all but 171 had EE traction equipment.

The only other shunters with EE equipment were the pair of identical prototypes of 500bhp built by English Electric and Vulcan Foundry in 1956; one had electric and the other a Krupp-type hydraulic transmission for comparison. Both were tried on BR, the diesel-electric version proving superior and putting in good service until 1960. As D0226 it may be found today on the Keighley & Worth Valley Light Railway.

Finally in 1965 six of the standard BR EE units were converted at Darlington into twin-unit 'master and slave' hump shunting locomotives for special use at Tinsley marshalling yard, Sheffield, and are still at work there.

CHAPTER 2

THE ENGLISH ELECTRIC DIESEL ENGINE RANGE

It is not an exaggeration to say that no other British rail traction oil engine has a longer history than that of the English Electric range, and it is possible, too, that no other engine range has given so little trouble to its operators for so long a period.

For over 40 years this 10in by 12in cylinder range—that is, from its first locomotive application in 1934—has retained many of its original characteristics. In 1934 it was a six-cylinder vertical engine of 300bhp, raised in 1935 to 350bhp, and later to 400bhp, which set the standard for the ubiquitous diesel-electric shunter of today, not only on BR, but on railways in many other countries.

The original English Electric six-cylinder locomotive diesel engine was built at Willans Rugby works. It had integrally-cast crankcase and cylinder block of iron, with pistons, liners, and cylinder heads of a special cast iron, and separate cylinder heads. The one-piece cast steel sump and bedplate was extended at one end to carry the main generator fan and to bolt to the generator casing.

The bearings were steel-shelled white-metal lined to carry the one-piece carbon steel crank-shaft. The camshaft was housed in the side of the crankcase, running in plain bearings, having a diameter larger than that of the cams so that the whole shaft could be moved in and out without touching the cams. The inlet and exhaust valve cams were in one piece and keyed to the shaft; the fuel valve cams were split and adjustable. The inlet and exhaust valves were driven in the usual way through push rods and rockers, being positively closed by double concentric springs, and the connecting rods were secured to the piston by fully floating gudgeon pins.

After the outbreak of war in 1939, the K range vertical engine was developed into a vee-form engine, turbo-charging was tried, and the two-valve was replaced by a four-valve cylinder head; speed was increased from 685 to 750rpm, later to 850rpm, and modifications included the use of tri-metal bearings, redesign of connecting rods, new fuel-injection equipment, charge-air cooling, strengthening of the crankcase and higher firing pressures.

For main line traction the vee engine was first produced in 12 cylinder form during 1945/6, being followed by six and eight cylinder vertical and 16 cylinder vee engines designed to take pressure-charging. The prototype engine was followed by a production batch of 16 cylinder vee engines of 1600bhp for use in some large 1A-Do-A1 locomotives for Egypt and LMS units Nos 10000/1. Engine construction, originally at the Willans works at Rugby, was moved to Preston, the Dick, Kerr, works, to be followed by Vulcan Foundry during the 1960s.

The first 16 cylinder engine, then classified 16KV, was tested at Rugby in the autumn of 1947. The official classification of SVT for the vee range was adopted, with SRKT for the vertical engines, all with pressure charging and a speed of 750rpm. The vee engine of 1947, used in LMS 10000/1 and the Egyptian locomotives, had the two-valve head and ran at 750rpm. By the time BR Nos 10201/2 were built, output had reached 1750bhp, still at 750rpm, in which form it was used in some South Australian locomotives; its first application at 2000bhp and 850rpm was on BR locomotives in 1954.

The 12 cylinder vee unit was not used in a production run until 1952 when in an order for Queensland it was set to give 1290bhp; it was later applied for the same railway and for Malayan Railways at 1500bhp, to be followed by the BR D6700 (Class 37) 1750bhp units, and, with pressure charging, 1840-2025bhp machines for Rhodesia, East Africa, and Sudan. The engine is a four-stroke unit with two banks of cylinders set at an angle of 45 degrees with opposite cylinders staggered so that plain side by side rods can be used. Of monobloc construction and fully enclosed, it has integrally-mounted lubricating oil and cooling water circulation pumps, gear driven from the crankshaft. Separate mechanical fuel injection pumps were provided for each cylinder, feeding into open-type combustion chambers.

The engine bedplate formed the lower halves of the main bearing housing, the bearing caps being positively locked into the bedplate; the solid mounting plate for the generator was at one end and the bedplate forms the lubricating oil sump. Resilient mounting for the engine/

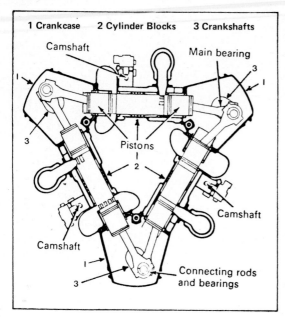

1 Crankcase   2 Cylinder Blocks   3 Crankshafts

Camshaft   Main bearing

Pistons

Camshaft

Camshaft

Connecting rods
and bearings

Fig 2: Diagram of layout of Napier Deltic opposed piston engine. *(GEC Traction Ltd)*

generator group left this free from the effects of underframe flexing and assisted in engine changing and lining-up processes.

The crankcase is a rigid unit with transverse diaphragms between the cylinders with compartments along both sides enclosing camshafts and tappets. Generous inspection doors permit big-end and main-bearing withdrawal while washout openings for flushing out cooling-water spaces are provided. Separate, wet-type cast iron cylinder liners held by top flanges at the cylinder head are fitted, the lower end being sealed by rings into the crankcase. Crankshaft main-bearings have steel shells and lead-bronze linings, renewal being possible without scraping or hand fitting; its proportions are arranged to obviate critical vibration speeds in its normal operating range.

The pistons, of aluminium-silicon alloy, give good heat transfer and maximum bearing surface. Three piston rings, the upper one chromium plated and placed well below the piston crown, are fitted, the crown having a bowl-shaped combustion chamber machined into it. Hollow, fully floating, case-hardened steel gudgeon pins are used. Piston removal was achieved by taking off the cylinder head and big-end cap and lifting out with the connecting rod

upwards through the cylinder liner. Big-end bearings are detachable steel shells lined with lead bronze; small-end bearings are steel bushes pressed into the eyes of the rods, lined with lead bronze.

The cylinder heads, individual alloy-iron castings, have water-cooled combustion chamber roof, port walls and fuel-injection sleeve, access for cleaning water spaces being provided. Long studs passing through the cylinder head and narrow joint ring between head and liner hold down the cylinder head on the flanged top of the liner.

Each head has two inlet and two exhaust valves of silicon-chrome steel, each loaded with two coil springs. The valve seatings have inserts of hardened steel-alloy pressed into the cylinder head. The valves are operated by lubricated followers from the cams, with hardened steel rollers and short stiff push rods operating drop forged valve levers and guided bridge pieces driving the valves in pairs.

The Napier pressure-chargers consist of single-stage exhaust-gas turbine and centrifugal compressor, both turbine and exhaust outlet casings being water-cooled. Single-stage compressors are fitted, which in the case of charge-air cooled engines, have water-cooled air, via a heat exchanger, delivered to them to reduce the temperature of the air fed to the cylinders. Charge-air cooled engines have two water circuits, each with its own radiator section.

Engine governors are mechanical, of English Electric type, with hydraulic servo gear, or the Woodward P. G. governor for operating the fuel pump control shaft, being driven by bevel gears from the camshaft. Both give full protection to the engine in the loss of oil pressure. Lubricating oil and water pumps are bevel gear driven from an auxiliary shaft driven from the crankshaft. The engine sump oil is pumped by an engine-driven pump, passed through a wire-mesh cleaner and oil cooler, and filtered before delivery to the various bearings.

Fuel is pressure delivered through a fabric filter to the bus rails serving the injection pumps, excess fuel being returned via a relief valve to the tank.

Charge-air cooling was first applied in export work to East Africa; its advantage is that it permits a much higher compression ratio on the turbo-charger and enables it to overcome air supply difficulties in engines operating at high altitudes. This obviated the practice of fitting large de-rated engines to achieve the requisite output.

In using charge-air cooling at low altitudes in cold conditions, the air supply must be kept within the limits of cylinder peak pressure to avoid mechanical overloading. The first work was carried out on the 12 cylinder engine, but more important work on the 16 cylinder unit, which finds use on BR in 2000/2700bhp sizes, was carried out.

Work with a prototype 16 cylinder engine, during which proving was carried up to 2920hp, was followed by an application in traction with prototype locomotive DP2. An important aspect of the continual development of this engine is the reduction in power/weight ratio between 1947 and 1963.

Original	16 SVT	1600bhp	24.1lb per bhp
Mark II	16 SVT	2000bhp	20.4lb per bhp
Mark III	16 CSVT	2700bhp	16.1lb per bhp

By 1969 further development in the RKT/VT range resulted in a completely new power capability, and by this time over 3000 engines were in worldwide use. Improved turbo-charging from a new Napier SA085 turbo-blower with plain bearings, oil-cooled pistons, induction hardened pins and journals on the CGF crankshaft and gear driven camshafts on the vee engines were major new features.

In spite of improvements, a high degree of component interchangeability was maintained with previous RKT/VT engines. Reduced maintenance costs were achieved by using spur-gear driven auxiliaries on all vee engines, high pressure fuel pipe connections outside the cylinder head covers, and the absence of flexible hose connections.

The Mark III English Electric engine range was then listed as:

Model	RPM	BHP (to BS 2953)
6SRKT	900	1050
6CSRKT	900	1320
8SVT	900	1400
8CSVT	900	1760
12SVT	900	2100
12CSVT	900	2640
16SVT	900	2800
16CSVT	900	3520

The latter engine was chosen by BR for 60 3520bhp Co-Co freight locomotives for delivery in 1976.

Also included in the English Electric group was the firm of D. Napier and Son, Ltd, manufacturers of the Deltic engine range. The Deltic engine is an opposed piston engine operating on the two-stroke cycle, employing either a mechanically-driven scavenge blower or a turbo-blower. Charge-air coolers were used in the higher rated engines, being integral with the turbo-blower unit. Although designed to meet navy requirements for marine installations, it is an obvious choice for rail application.

The triangular arrangement of the 18 cylinders results in a compact engine consisting of three cylinder blocks forming the sides, and three crankcases, one at each apex of the triangle. This arrangement fully exploits the mechanical simplicity of the opposed piston design. Short crankshafts are used, and, as each crankpin carries one inlet and one exhaust piston, the loading on all crankpins is identical, and the reciprocating forces are balanced within the engine. The power transmitted through each crankshaft is identical, and torsional vibration is controlled by the use of quill shafts in tune with dampers secured to each crankshaft.

The Deltic engine comprises four main assemblies: the main triangle, phasing gear, blower unit, and the integral gearbox or an end-cover assembly. The main triangle comprises three cylinder blocks and three crankcases tied together by high tensile steel bolts passing through the cylinder blocks and crankcases. These through-bolts carry the combustion loads and unite the whole assembly into a structure of great strength and rigidity.

The cylinder blocks, each carrying six cylinder liners, are identical light alloy castings with integral air-inlet manifolds, coolant galleries and exhaust ports. Wet type cylinder liners, machined from hollow steel forgings, are chromium plated for long life with oil retaining surfaces. Each liner is encircled by four annular cooling spaces, the exhaust port bars being cooled by co-axial holes drilled through the bars and interconnecting two of the annular cooling spaces. A flange at the inlet end of the liner seats on a shoulder in the cylinder block to provide longitudinal location, the assembly being secured by a ringnut.

Each crankcase is also a one-piece light-alloy casting substantially webbed and carrying a crankshaft in thin-walled, lead bronze, lead plated, indium infused main bearings. The main bearing caps are each secured by four studs being located additionally by a tie-bolt which passes transversely through the cap and crankcase walls. The two upper crankcases are identical in construction, but the lower one is deeper in section to provide a sump for drain oil for the 'dry sump' lubrication system.

Crankshafts are machined from forgings and have six throws and seven main journals with all bearing surfaces finished by lapping. Each crankshaft is fitted with a viscous type torsional vibration damper. The two top crankshafts are identical and rotate in a clockwise direction when viewed from the free-end. The bottom crankshaft has opposite handed throws, and rotates in an anti-clockwise direction so that the correct phase relationship is achieved.

Each crankpin carries a pair of connecting rods, one forked and one plain, manufactured from drop-forgings machined and polished all over. Each exhaust piston is attached to a forked rod with a steel shell at the large end. The inner surface of the shell has a thin-wall bearing for the crankpin. Each inlet piston is attached to a plain rod, the large end having a thin-wall bearing. The plain rod is supported on the steel bearing shell between the legs of the forked rod.

The pistons have an outer body and a gudgeon pin housing. The outer body has a copper-alloy crown attached to a Y alloy skirt. Two rings are fitted in the crown and three oil rings in the skirt.

No valve gear is used in the Deltic engine; the three forged camshafts, only being required to drive the fuel injection pumps, are carried in alloy castings on each cylinder block. Each is driven through a train of gears and a short quill-shaft.

An opposed-piston engine has its three crank-shafts geared together to maintain the correct phase relationship. A phasing gear train, to which the crankshafts are coupled by quill shafts, is coupled to a common output shaft. A machined face on the phasing gear casing is designed to take a flange-mounted generator.

The Deltic engines, with their advantages of light weight and compactness, combined with high power output, were not only capable of use in high-power, lightweight locomotives, but with unit-replacement maintenance, in which an engine is lifted out and another put in, reduced the time the locomotive was out of service.

TABLE 1

TOTALS OF ENGLISH ELECTRIC DIESEL ENGINES SUPPLIED FOR USE IN ENGLISH ELECTRIC EQUIPPED AND ENGLISH ELECTRIC BUILT DIESEL ELECTRIC LOCOMOTIVES OWNED BY BRITISH MAIN LINE RAILWAYS 1934-1975

List excludes spare engines, prototype 500 bhp shunters, electro-diesel locomotives, diesel-electric railcars, and engines supplied to re-engine other makers' locomotives

Engine Model	Power Range (BHP)	Delivery Period	No of Engines	Locos to which fitted
6KT.	300/350/400	1934-1962	1233	0-6-0DE shunters
8SVT	1000	1957-1968	228	Class 20
12CSVT	1750	1960-1965	309	Class 37
16 SVT	1600/1750/ 2000	1947-1962	205	10000/1 10201-3 Class 40
16CSVT	2700	1962-1968	51	DP2* Class 50
T9-29	1100	1959	10	Class 23
D18-25	1650	1955-1962	46	Prototype Deltic* Class 55

Total Engines 2082

Notes: * Locomotives owned by English Electric and loaned to BR.
** Locomotives owned by English Electric and leased to BR

CHAPTER 3

THE FIRST STEPS:
10000 AND 10001 ON THE LMR: 1947–1953

Shortly after the end of hostilities the SR, LMS, and LNER all expressed interest in main line diesel-electric traction, the exception, of course, being the GWR, which decided to try gas turbine traction in furtherance of Swindon's traditional 'go-it-alone' attitude. All these plans were to be applauded, for at last it seemed that the British main line railways were moving away from their traditional steam traction approach.

The SR was first in the arena when, in the late autumn of 1946 it decided to build three 1600bhp diesel-electric locomotives for West of England passenger services. The origin of the SR Board's decision stemmed from 1945 when a party of senior officials visited the USA to study diesel traction use. Their findings, set out in a report, were recommended to the Board by the SR's General Manager Sir Eustace Missenden.

Financial priorities played their part in holding up the project, and it was not until after nationalisation, in 1950, that the first locomotive was built. It is worth recording that this scheme originated well before that of the LMS, and design work was carried on quite independently.

The LMS made its announcement to try main line diesel-electric traction in early 1947, envisaging three units of two types, one of 800bhp to undertake branch and cross-country services and two larger 1600bhp locomotives which could be used singly on medium mixed-traffic work, or in multiple as a 3200bhp unit on the heaviest Anglo-Scottish duties. Moreover, the LMS announced that trials would be staged against its Duchess Pacifics, two new ones being built with a number of detail improvements on earlier examples to provide modern steam locomotives with which to compare the diesel units. The interesting feature of the SR and LMS plans was that the English Electric Co, Ltd was to supply all the 1600bhp traction equipment.

LNER plans for diesel traction, made public in mid-1947, were more ambitious in envisaging no fewer than 25 1600bhp locomotives, for the Anglo-Scottish services of the East Coast route, operating as 3200bhp multiple units. They were to be capable of 100mph running, and in this respect, and in proposals for new diesel depots at Edinburgh and near Holloway in London, also the expectation that the new diesel-electrics would release 32 Pacifics for other duties, pre-dated the later thinking of BR. The LNER plans did not in fact go ahead.

Meanwhile, the GWR pressed ahead with its gas turbine projects, and ordered two machines for trials, one from Switzerland by Brown-Boveri/Swiss Locomotive Company, and one from Metropolitan-Vickers Ltd in the UK, both outside of our scope here.

The first locomotives to appear were the two LMS units from Derby works, the first, No 10000, being finished in late November 1947, only seven months from the drawing board to delivery in running order, so keen was the LMS to finish one before nationalisation.

Although acclaimed as the first British main line diesel locomotives, this was quite inaccurate, for the honour goes to the Tyneside company of Sir W. G. Armstrong, Whitworth & Co, Ltd which had a diesel traction department from 1931 until 1938. This company built 25 diesel-electric units for British use alone, not to mention exports, its first British main line unit being completed in 1933, described in *British Internal Combustion Locomotive, 1894-1940*. This was an 800bhp 1-Co-1 diesel-electric mixed-traffic unit, which ran over 26,000 miles on the LNER main lines in the North East, and into Scotland, during 1933/4. At all times it remained its maker's property, so perhaps the 1947 LMS units could claim to be the first main line diesels built for a British main line railway.

LMS 10000, painted black, with raised numbers, LMS initials, waistband, and roof in silver, was a Co-Co unit of 121½ tons service weight, with the twin cab/nose configuration traditionally expected of a diesel locomotive. Although produced under the aegis of H. G. Ivatt, then LMS chief mechanical engineer, the influence of English Electric in the design was very great. It is interesting to note in passing that English Electric itself, at the same time as Derby was occupied on this project, was engaged on its first post-war main line diesel-electric locomotives, a batch of 12 1A-Do-A1 standard gauge units for Egypt, using the same engine as the LMS locomotives, indeed, from the same production batch, at Preston Works and Vulcan Foundry.

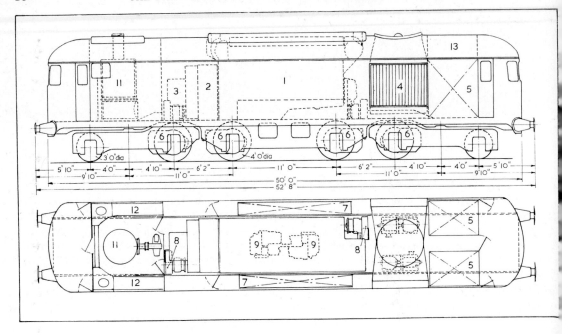

Above: **Fig 3**: Derby works of the LMS had development work in progress during the period when C. E. Fairburn was chief mechanical engineer, on English Electric powered main line diesel-electrics. One, a 1600bhp 16SVT engined 1A-Bo-A1, would have weighed 107 tons in working order, and had its centre pair of axles in a rigid frame structure, but with bogies at the outer ends. It was a very different concept to the locomotives built under Ivatt.

Right: No 10000 on a test train between Derby and Manchester in 1948. *(GEC Traction Ltd)*

Below: **Fig 4**: Side elevation of LMS Co-Co diesel-electric locomotive No 10000, built at Derby in 1947, the first main line DE locomotive owned by a British main line railway. *(Author's collection)*

The mechanical design of 10000 and 10001 was based on I section main longitudinals braced by cross-stretchers, forming a foundation for the power-equipment, the whole being decked over with aluminium floor plates sealed to prevent oil and water contamination to under-gear and bogies.

The superstructure comprised a centre assembly between the inner cab bulkheads, mounted on pivots to prevent stress damage by underframe flexing and was removable without affecting the cab/nose units. The centre roof section had hinged doors for access, maintenance, and inspection and removable hatches permitted the engine to be lifted out.

Driving cab layouts at each end were identical, all controls being readily to hand; they

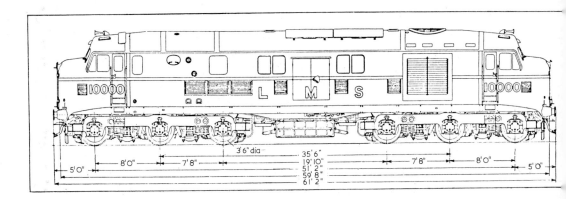

included an eight-notch controller giving engine speeds of 450, 630 and 750rpm in conjunction with varying degrees of excitation of generator field, the eighth notch giving full throttle. Other controls were the vacuum-brake valve fed by a pair of Westinghouse exhausters, windscreen wiper/washer, sanding and warning horn, defrosters, and sunblinds. A deadman's pedal was fitted at the driving position, and a hand-brake wheel at the secondman's seat. Indirect illumination of instruments and full warning lights were fitted.

The nose-compartments contained traction motor blowers and the air-compressor, a flexible gangway to permit inter-locomotive access when operating in multiple or to the leading coach of the train.

The central section of the locomotive, in addition to the engine/generator set, housed the cooling radiators and associated roof-mounted fan, control cubicle, service and main fuel tanks, coolant and train-heating water tanks, train-heating fuel tank, toilet, auxiliary generator, and a Clarkson thimble-tube train-heating boiler. The latter were boilers rather than steam-generators and were lit by poking in a piece of burning cotton waste. By the mid 1950s both locomotives were fitted with Spanner train-heating boilers, and the fuel supply arranged so that it drew from the main locomotive fuel tank. The removal of the boiler fuel tank allowed a larger water tank to be installed. Battery boxes

and vacuum brake cylinders were both hung from the underframe.

The bogies had sandwich-type main frames with equalising beams resting on top of the Timken roller-bearing axle-boxes, twin-bolsters giving good riding qualities. The bolsters were original in having a non-rigid coupling arrangement to take the weight of the locomotive body. This put the weight on the axes of the bolsters via sliding surfaces, leaving the bogie pivot to deal with location and traction forces only. This system, using a lighter connecting member to join centre-pivot to bolsters, gave sufficient clearance within the bogie for the centre-axle traction motor.

The engine was the English Electric 16 SVT 16 cylinder vee unit rated at 1600bhp/750rpm, being fitted with four British Brown-Boveri turbo-chargers, each serving four cylinders. The English Electric main generator, directly coupled to the engine, was a single-bearing, self-ventilated unit continuously rated at 1080kW at 650V, 1660amp. Two separately-excited field windings and a series decompounding winding were provided, the latter for use when motoring the main generator for engine starting.

The shunt-wound auxiliary generator over-hung from the main generator was rated continuously at 50kW, 135V, 375amp, and supplied power for control circuits, excitation of the generator fields, battery charging, driving

compressors, exhausters, traction motor blowers, locomotive lighting. The radiator fan was driven by a vertical drive motor from the main generator.

Each of the six English Electric nose-suspended, axle-hung, force-ventilated, series wound, single reduction gear drive traction motors had a continuous weak field rating of 220hp, 300V, 500amp and were connected in three parallel groups of two motors in series.

Twin Serck radiators, consisting of headers and oil and water cooling elements, were fitted one each side of the cooling compartment and were thermostatically and manually controlled for temperature, the latter by shutters. Cooling air was drawn in by the roof-mounted fan through the sides and expelled via the roof. Air for combustion came in via bodyside Vokes filters.

Air-tight doors separated the compartment containing the control cubicle from the engine room, the main and auxiliary generators projecting through the associated bulkhead and drawing their air through Vokes bodyside filters.

10000 was tested from Derby during December 1947, and sent to Euston for official

No 10001 on the Camden fitted freight duty during winter months in 1949 and 1950, seen near Tring. (C. R. L. Coles)

Inspection along with new Pacific No 6256 *Sir William A. Stanier, FRS,* both being allocated to Camden shed, on 18 December, 10000 returning to Derby for further trials. Following dynamometer car trials between Derby and Trent it was sent out on its first long run on 14/15 January 1948 with 12 coaches and a dynamometer car taring 393 tons, equal to a 5XP (Jubilee) 4-6-0 loading on the Midland line, arriving at St Pancras 3min early. On the return run the next day 10000 took the train to Manchester Central on a typical service schedule. The 4½ mile Millers Dale-Peak Forest section, with three miles at 1 in 90 was covered in 8min start to pass, or with 2min in hand, and this lead was maintained until arrival at Manchester.

Following modifications at Derby, including stronger fuel tanks, tests to Trent, and training runs with braking and train-heating trials, 10000 was put on Derby-St Pancras passenger duties from 23 February, involving a round trip of 257 miles daily, working the 08.55 up and 14.15 down with loads of 390 tons. The running was extended on 15 March by adding an evening Derby-Manchester round trip, giving 10000 a rise in six-day weekly mileage from 1542 to 2268.

From 6 April the duty was altered to two round trips between Derby and St Pancras, raising the six day mileage to 3084. 10000 had time and power in hand on 5XP Jubilee 4-6-0 timings, the pre-war 99min St Pancras-Leicester schedules being well within its capacity.

10001 was completed in July 1948 in the same livery, but without the LMS initials, and it too was allocated to Camden, but loaned to Derby. 10001 took on 10000's duties, the latter entering Derby works with a mileage of 51,300 for inspection.

October 1948 saw both move to Camden for trials and training before taking up West Coast main line duties. Their first long runs in multiple took place on 4/5 October. On the 5th, with the 13.00 Euston-Glasgow, the pair took the train as far as Carlisle, with 16 coaches,

No 10001 pilots 10000 in multiple on a Perth express at Moore near Warrington on 4 June 1949. *(Harold D. Bowtell)*

496/530 tons tare/gross, to Crewe, where a four-coach Blackpool portion was detached, leaving 368/390 tons. A full-throttle start from Euston saw the 785 tons load (including locomotives) climb the 1 in 70/105/77 Camden bank to its summit reaching 33mph, continuing to pass South Hampstead, 2.4 miles, in 4min 45sec at 60mph. The train reached Rugby in 86½min, and Crewe, 158.1 miles, in 176min, against schedules of 93 and 183min respectively. Further north, 10000/1 reached 78mph at the foot of the 12½ miles Grayrigg Bank, while Tebay, 31.1 miles from Morecambe South Junction, was passed in 30min at 65mph, and Scout Green box on Shap's 1 in 75 was passed at 49mph. On arrival at Carlisle the 68 miles from Morecambe South Junction had taken 67min 15sec. The pair continued this duty for five days until 10000 failed and went to Derby for attention.

Both locomotives were transferred to Willesden shed at the end of 1948, but while 10000 was in works, 10001 was also at Derby on Midland line duties, both remaining there until May 1949. In the summer they were on West Coast Anglo-Scottish trains as far as Carlisle, a main activity being the 10.00 Euston-Glasgow Royal Scot, giving a 24 hour mileage of 600. On one such run, 1 June, the Royal Scot was specially arranged to run non-stop from Euston to Glasgow; the train, including a 12-wheel dining car and open-first for guests, weighed 520/545 tons tare/gross and had a total length, including locomotives, of 1008ft, much longer than Euston's platform 13. This ably demonstrated the bulk of multiple operation with low-powered diesels.

With a locomotive weight in multiple of 255 tons, 100 tons more than a Duchess Pacific, and a point seized on immediately by steam die-hards, the bulk made no difference, as it was all adhesive weight and gave a starting tractive effort of 82,800 lb, double that of a Duchess!

Without banking assistance 10000/1 made a rapid exit to pass Camden No 1 box at the top of the bank, 1.1 miles in 2min 32sec at 30mph. Watford Junction was passed in 20min 55sec for 17½ miles, 3min early and exactly on the pre-war Royal Scot schedule, even with a 545 tons tail load! Because the run was designed to be non-stop much time-filling was needed to avoid signal checks. The train passed Rugby 82.6 miles in 87½min, 4½min early. North of Crewe full throttle running from Milnthorpe saw Grayrigg Bank, in 104/131, topped at

49/53mph and in spite of a slowing to 30mph at
Tebay, Shap was climbed at 41/34/33mph, the
31.4 miles from Carnforth having taken 41min
12sec, 38min net. North of Carlisle, Gretna was
passed 9½min early, while on Beattock, with 1
in 88/80/74/75, speeds of 51/44/37/33/33½
were recorded, the climb taking 16min 25sec
against a schedule of 22min. Glasgow was finally
reached 3min early.

Mileage figures for 10000/1 in multiple
between 10 July-14 August was 20,874, or equal
to a round Euston-Glasgow trip for 35 consecutive days.

During the autumn, single-unit haulage of
390/440 tons Euston-Blackpool trains by 10000,
460 miles round trips, demonstrated the
capacity of one unit on heavy work.

Because of the unreliability of train-heating
equipment, 10000/1 found themselves on freight
haulage in winter months, mostly on Camden-
Crewe vacuum-fitted freight with 40-50 wagon
loadings, and with maximum speeds of about
50mph, regearing was necessary to permit long
periods of operation at lower speeds. Eight to
12min early arrivals were common on this work.

The diesel twins were not permitted on the
G & SWR route via Kilmarnock, so their
running north of the border was always on the
Caledonian main line. 10001 spent late 1949/
early 1950 in works, and it was not until May
that they returned to Anglo-Scottish duties.

During that summer in multiple they worked
the 21.05 Euston-Glasgow sleeper of up to 545
tons weight, returning next day with the up
Royal Scot, giving a daily mileage of 803. In just
over four months they put in 69,213 train miles.

Early 1951 saw 10001 receive its first heavy
repair and repaint; both were active on the
Midland line in March, but April saw them on
the West Coast again. During 6-9 June, 10001
was tried singly on Euston-Glasgow trains:

6 June 10.00 Euston-Glasgow { 475 tons tare to Carlisle / 330 tons tare to Glasgow
7 June 22.10 Glasgow-Euston   517 tons tare
8/9 June 21.10 Euston-Glasgow { 498 tons tare / 530 tons gross
9 June 10.00 Glasgow-Euston { 473 tons tare / 510 tons gross

One unit was found able to handle these
loadings and run to schedule in spite of severe
delays, running with time in hand on easy
sections, but losing time on the hills. The run of
9 June is set out here briefly:

	Distance miles	Schedule mins	Actual mins	Net Time mins
Glasgow-Carlisle	102.3	125	134	122½
Carlisle-Euston	299.1	361	368	318
Totals	401.4	486*	502	440½

* Average speed 49.6mph
**Average speed 54.7mph

After visits to works they were both put to
work on Crewe, Liverpool and Blackpool trains
singly from Euston with average loadings of
450 tons gross, some rosters involving 703 miles
daily and giving 10001 a four-monthly mileage
of over 38,000 during the summer of 1951.

Their somewhat meandering employment by
the LMR provokes the thought to enquire why
were they never tried on the Edinburgh-
Aberdeen route of the East Coast? This line with
its heavy loadings for principal trains, and
severe line gradients and curvature, would have
been ideal for multiple operation, their 255 tons
adhesive weight and 37,000lb continuous one
hour rated tractive effort.

10000 lost its LMS initials in mid-1951 and by
1952, their trial period over, they took on any
odd steam duties available, not the vogue for any
main line diesel locomotive. Hope came when
they were transferred during March/April 1953
to the SR to join 10201/2 on West of England
duties. To comply with SR loading gauge
limitations both locomotives were reduced
slightly in overall width by detail alterations to
air-intakes, handrails etc; the SR six-position
headcode marker light system was fitted.

TABLE 2
**MAIN DETAILS AND DIMENSIONS OF
LOCOMOTIVES 10000/1**

Description	Data
Axle layout	Co-Co
Engine model	16SVT
Engine rating	1600BHP at 750rpm
Locomotive weight, in working order	127 tons 13cwt
Brakes, locomotive	Vacuum
Brakes, train	Vacuum
Train heating	Clarkson boiler/later Spanner boiler
Boiler water tank capacity	600gals
Length over buffers	61ft 2in
Overall width	9ft 3in
Overall height	12ft 11½in
Wheel diameter	3ft 6in
Bogie wheelbase	15ft 8in
Total wheelbase	51ft 2in
Bogie pivots	35ft 6in
Maximum speed	93mph
Maximum tractive effort	41,400 lb
Continuous tractive effort	15,000 lb at 32mph
Locomotive and boiler fuel capacity	890gals

CHAPTER 4

10201–3 AND 10000/1: 1950–1966

The three SR 1Co-Co1 diesel-electrics were conceived before the LMS units, but did not appear until four years after them, having a more profound effect on future BR diesel traction. The southern units, 10201-3, were the products of the collaboration of O. V. S. Bulleid, the SR CME, and C. M. Cock, Chief Electrical Engineer, being responsible for mechanical and electrical design, respectively, although S. B. Warder supervised their construction as the Southern Region Mechanical & Electrical Engineer after Bulleid's retirement.

The first two locomotives were put in hand at Ashford works in 1949, but the third was deferred to permit some re-design after experience with 10201/2. 10201 was in an advanced stage at Ashford in mid-1950, but was not ready until late November, when it ran initial trials to Wye, Dover, and Ramsgate. In early January 1951 it went to Derby works and ran trials on the Midland line. Monday, 8 January, saw 10201 on Derby-St Pancras passenger trains, continuing until the 17th, when it went back to Ashford works for preparation as an exhibit for the 1951 Festival of Britain. In spite of its SR origin, the LMR saw fit to apply its 'divine right' in adding it to its running stock in January, but on loan to the SR!

Mechanically 10201 was quite traditionally constructed, but was interesting in not having the usual nose, in fact the flat front was to be a pointer to BR practice of 10 years later.

The underframe had two inner I sections and two outer channel sections braced with steel plate and rolled sections to support the heavier items of equipment; light steel top and bottom plates gave additional strength in the centre. The bodyside contours followed that of current SR coaching stock, being of light steel panelling riveted to a rolled steel framework; only the roof top access doors were of alloy. Like 10000/1 the centre section between the cabs was mounted on Silentbloc bearings to absolve it from underframe flexing. The body sides were detachable for engine removal if required.

The driving cabs were double-panelled for insulation and had, together with the generator compartment, a wooden floor. Bogie design was based on plate side-frames made rigid by cross-stretchers, two in the middle carrying the

segmental bearings; dragboxes built into the outer ends of the frame carried the two spring-loaded side bearers.

The leading wheels of each bogie were purely for guiding and in the form of pony trucks anchored by two pairs of short links ahead of the axle to the buffer beam. The links had spherical bearings with side-play controlled by springs. Cannon type bearings were used for the pony axles.

The driven axles had Timken roller-bearing axle-boxes, only the centre one having side-play allowance, the others nominal play. Laminated springing and auxiliary coil and rubber springing were used on axle-boxes and links, respectively.

The engine, identical to those of 10000/1, was the English Electric 16 SVT unit rated at 1600bhp continuously or 1750bhp for one hour at 750rpm. Four Napier exhaust-gas turbo-blowers gave the pressure-charging. CAV fuel injection was used. Engine speed was variable from 435rpm idling through 600rpm intermediate, and 750rpm maximum.

Cooling water circulation was by two engine-driven centrifugal pumps. The radiators were bodyside mounted and had two vertical panels of Serck elements with oil and water sections, the air being drawn in and through the radiators by a roof-mounted, motor-driven fan, air flow being controlled by shutters. To ensure an adequate supply of oil at engine starting, a motor-driven priming pump was fitted. Engine starting was by motoring the main generator as a series motor from the batteries.

An English Electric type EE823a main generator with a single bearing directly coupled to the engine crankshaft was used. It was a dc eight-pole machine with self-ventilation, two separately excited field windings and a series decompounding winding for engine starting. The generator shaft was extended to take the overhung auxiliary generator, rated at 1155kW, 1650amp, at 700V continuously.

Control equipment was housed in a central frame behind No 2 cab. The main traction motor and field weakening contactors were electro-pneumatic; full use of engine power was controlled by a load regulator.

Nose-suspended, axle-hung, series-wound

traction motors of English Electric type 519/4D were used, driving through a single-reduction 52:21 ratio gearing to the axles. They were connected in series pairs across the main generator, with individual windings for 400V nominal. One or more motors could be cut out, the locomotive being operable on the remainder. Force-ventilation by motor-driven fans, one to each bogie, was fitted.

The traction motor continuous rating was 220hp each, 460amp, 400V and one hour rating 260hp, 550amp, 400V. Air braking on the locomotive was controlled by a self-lapping valve; vacuum equipment was provided for the train. Motor-driven compressors were fitted under the locomotive, and a Westinghouse vacuum exhauster. Train-heating came from a Spanner Spiraflow oil-fired boiler.

With 10201 occupied at the Festival of Britain, attention was expectantly shifted to the progress with 10202 at Ashford. Testing was carried out in August similar to that of 10201 and the new locomotive went to Nine Elms shed for driver training.

In black and silver livery, like 10000/1 and 10201, it first appeared on the Western Section on 25 September 1951 on the 11.54 Waterloo-Salisbury, following this by about two weeks on Exeter line duties. From 15 October, 10202 was on the first stage of a 687mile daily diagram involving two round trips, Waterloo-Exeter.

Like 10201 before it, 10202 was again snatched by the LMR which allocated it to Derby shed in November 1951, although, of course, on loan to the SR; in practice it was not to operate on LMR metals at all for five years. On high-speed trials on 24 October 10202, with eight coaches, 261 tons tare, attempted the Salisbury-Waterloo run of 83¾ miles in 90min including a 5min stop at Andover Junction. The schedule and actual running was as follows:

	Miles	Schedule mins	Actual mins
Salisbury-Andover Jcn	17.3	22	22
Andover Jcn-Waterloo	66.2	63	61min 51se

A top speed of 87mph was attained near Hook and an average of 85mph Oakley-Farnborough

The 687 mile daily diagram was first operated on 29 October 1951, with the 01.25/13.00 Waterloo-Exeter and 07.30/17.53 return. 10202 performed excellently with nine to eleven coach loadings, being joined in early 1952 by 10201 released from the Festival of Britain in late November. 10202 meanwhile, apart from its three-monthly examinations, held the fort on the Exeter services. Both units were in Brighton works in February, following which they took on the Waterloo-Weymouth, Waterloo-Exeter on weekdays and Bournemouth/Southampton/

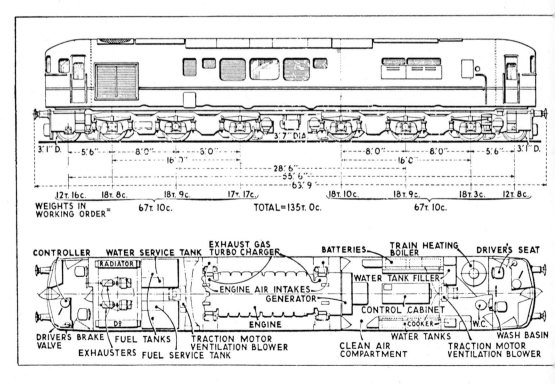

Yeovil duties on Sundays, including the Bournemouth Belle. By this time, 10202 had recorded 85,000 miles in service.

10201/2 were each taking 14 coach loads with ease during the summer of 1952, and it may be noted that their consistent performances totally eclipsed those of 10000/1 with their recorded 800 miles daily on the Royal Scot, the two SR units doing 687 miles per day, not just for short periods, but for five months.

The locomotives were able to pass Byfleet Junction, 19½ miles from Waterloo, in under 20 minutes, with 331/350 ton loads, at speeds in the 70s. The rising gradients of 1 in 326/314/300 after Woking presented no

Above: In new condition, the second Ashford-built 1750bhp 1Co-Co1 DE 10202 is seen at Woking in 1951. *(GEC Traction Ltd)*

Left: **Fig 5**: Diagram of SR 1750bhp 1Co-Co1 DE units 10201/2 built at Ashford in 1950/1. *(Author's collection)*

Below: Strangers at Waterloo on 21 June 1953. LMR locomotive No 10000 waiting with the 13.00 to Exeter and ER class V2 2-6-2 No 60917 on loan to cover the temporary withdrawal of SR Pacifics. *(R. C. Riley)*

problems, nor the 1 in 249 approaching Basingstoke, up which speeds of 70mph were common. The fastest running often took place before Salisbury, with 86-90mph a frequent attainment. With a mileage of 89,270 and engine hours of 2680, 10202 was put on service trials with a dynamometer car on 28-30 April/1 May 1952 on the Waterloo-Exeter line, involving the 13.00 from Waterloo, with loadings of 265 tons (eight coaches) to 432 tons (13 coaches), returning on the 19.30 ex Exeter.

They were followed on 28-31 October 1952 between Salisbury and Exeter also with 10202. By this time the locomotive had had an intermediate overhaul at Brighton at a mileage point of 100,880 miles, 3025 engine hours. The work included tyre-turning and re-gearing, but the diesel engine had only four pistons withdrawn for examination, no parts were replaced, nor was decarbonisation carried out, and by the October tests the mileage and engine hours were 130,310 and 3890, respectively.

The tests to ascertain tractive effort were carried out with a dynamometer car and loads of one, two, five, and eleven coaches. The re-gearing of the locomotives gave them an increase in maximum tractive effort to 48,000 lb at

24

SR 2000bhp diesel-electric No 10203 passes Bickley
Junction on 19 March 1955 during its brief trials on the
Golden Arrow. *(S. C. Nash)*

8.75mph and 21,700 lb at 24.5mph. The ratio of
the gears was 65:17 and permitted a top speed of
85mph, which proved more suitable than the
original gearing. During the tests drawbar
thermal efficiencies/fuel consumption per
drawbar-horsepower-hour (DBHP) at coasting
and braking periods in addition to underload
were tested.

By early 1953 Brighton works had started on
the third locomotive which, in spite of reports,
turned out to be very similar to 10201/2, except
to be of higher power. At this time 10201/2 were
joined at Nine Elms shed by those fugitives from
the LMR, 10000/1, giving four main line diesels
for West of England duties. In fact, 10000
arrived before 10001 which was in Derby works
in February/March, not reaching the SR until
April. At long last the LMR saw fit to transfer
10000/1, 10201/2 to SR stock during the
4 March-26 May accounting period.

The build-up of the Nine Elms diesel fleet
coincided with a difficult period for the SR
locomotives' reliability, their first non-scheduled
break for about 18 months on Exeter line duties.
10000/1 were given Waterloo-Exeter/Wey-
mouth/Bournemouth diagrams, but did not
perform at all satisfactorily in the summer of
1953.

On 8 February 1954, 10202, manned by Dover
crews, began work on the SR Eastern Section on
the up and down London-Paris Night Ferry and
Golden Arrow, doing so until the 14th, when it
returned to Nine Elms. After an absence of six
months 10000/1 returned to intermittent duty in
February 1954 before resuming Exeter
workings.

10203 was completed at Brighton in early
March 1954 and allocated to Nine Elms in April.
Following trials during April, it was exhibited at
the International Railway Congress Exhibition
of rolling stock at Willesden shed between
25 May and 4 June. Externally 10203 was very
similar to 10201/2, and had the same livery. It
was lighter in weight, at 132.8 tons compared
with 135 tons, while its starting tractive effort
was 50,000 lb, compared with 48,000 lb of
10201/2 after regearing in 1952. Apart from not
having end gangway doors for inter-locomotive
access as on 10201/2, the mechanical design was
the same, as were the controls, consisting of two

handles, the main power controller which
automatically gave full control of the engine
throttle and electrical equipment, and the
master switch handle both interlocked. The
latter had four positions: off, forward, engine
only, and reverse; the former gave infinitely
variable, notchless power output control.

The control equipment had electro-pneumatic
and electro-magnetic unit group switches. This
permitted the utilisation at all speeds of the full
power output, allowed function at all fractional
loads, and prevented overloading of the engine,
as well as automatically controlling the field
weakening of the traction motors. Other
controls and instrumentation included brake
handles for air/vacuum, warning horn, sanding
gear, deadman's pedal, main ammeter, brake
cylinder pressure gauge, air-pressure gauge,
steam-heating pressure gauge, vacuum gauge,
speedometer, push button engine starters and
exhauster control, together with indicator lights
for water temperature, oil-pressure, wheel slip,
train-heating boiler on, fire alarm, and were very
similar to those of 10201/2.

The engine was the latest version of the
English Electric 16 SVT engine in its Mark II
form, giving 2000bhp at 850rpm. The main
generator input was 1880bhp and four Napier
TS100/4 turbo-pressure chargers were fitted.

taking in air through body-side filters.

The generator, of type EE822/1B, was a ten-pole machine directly coupled to the engine; the outer end, as in 10201/2, carried the 48kW, 135V, 356amp, 850rpm auxiliary generator. The main generator's continuous rating was 1750amp, and maximum voltage 965.

The six, six-pole, series-wound, force-ventilated, axle-hung traction motors were permanently connected in series-parallel, in three groups of two in series, each group being fed current through a separate motor contactor. Three stage field weakening, minimum 25 per cent, by non-inductive shunt, was provided. The single-reduction spur gear drive had a ratio of 19:61. 10203 carried 1180gals of fuel oil, 16 gals lubricating oil, and water supplies of 280gals and 840gals for engine cooling and train-heating, respectively; the weight of supplies was about ten tons. The train-heating boiler was a BR-Laidlaw, Drew unit. Bogie design was similar to 10201/2, but braking was by Westinghouse straight-air and Westinghouse vacuum, the latter with Reavell twin-speed rotary exhausters.

During the summer of 1954 four out of five diesels were usually at work, while the superior power of 10203 soon became apparent in the way it could handle 13 coach trains on such

sections as Exeter-Yeovil Junction, 48¾ miles, in 55min. The winter of 1954/5 was to be their last on the SR and was a period of low availability, with only 10001 at work in early 1955. 10001 was transferred back to the LMR in February and put to work on Euston-Bletchley local trains; meanwhile 10000 and 10203 were again at work on the SR in March, during which month, from 13 March, the latter spent a week on the Night Ferry/Golden Arrow as had 10202 during 1954.

10000, 10201/2 were moved to the LMR during the four weeks ending 23 April 1955, joining 10001 at Willesden shed, and were soon at work on West Coast and Manchester duties. At the end of April both the up and down Royal Scot were in the charge of 10201/2 working singly.

Only 10203 was to remain on the SR, and during June/July 1955 it was subjected to a series of performance and efficiency tests, at the start of which it had a recorded mileage of 106,000 miles and 2865 engine hours. During the period 28 June-1 July it ran on controlled road tests, similar to those evolved by Swindon for its steam locomotive testing work, between Salisbury and Exeter, with loadings of between 63 and 392 tons including dynamometer car, or two to twelve coaches. They were followed by

revenue-earning tests, with dynamometer car included, between Waterloo and Exeter on 4-7 July. The test showed that 10203 in top controller position, with an engine output of 1883bhp at 850rpm, fuel rate of 752 lb/hour, had drawbar horsepowers of 1440 at 30mph, 1400 at 50mph, 1200 at 70mph, and 700 at 90mph, with equivalent tractive efforts of 26,800 lb at 20mph, 18,000 lb at 30 mph, 10,500 lb at 50mph, 6,600 lb at 70mph, and 2,800 lb, at 90mph. 10203 was moved to the LMR at Willesden on 20 July, being taken into stock in the third week in August.

The summer found 10000/1 on Anglo-Scottish duties, 10201/2 on Wolverhampton and Manchester services interspaced by long absences and periods on Bletchley locals. Following attention at Derby works, 10203 was put on the 00.20 Euston-Glasgow and 13.30 up Midday Scot involving a 24 hour mileage of 800 during September 1955. The following year saw all five locomotives spending long periods in Derby works during which 10000/1, 10201/2 lost their black and silver liveries for a dress of the drab BR olive green and cream numbers and roofs. Their visits to Derby almost always saw

them doing spells of duty on the Midland line.

Late 1956/early 1957 saw 10000/1 in multiple on Euston-Perth services and the Royal Scot and 10201/2 on one of their rare multiple workings saw service on the latter in early 1957. In March 1957 up to four and often five diesels were at work on Bletchley, Wolverhampton, Manchester, and Anglo-Scottish duties. The 20-30th of that month saw 10203 single-handed on the down Royal Scot, followed by 10000/1 and 10201/2 in multiple, while 10203 took on the Mancunian with odd appearances on the Royal Scot during April/May; 1957 nevertheless was to be the last year of notable employment for these five units. The end of the year found them all liveried in green, but with detail differences: 10000, silver line; 10001, white numbers, duck egg blue line; 10201-3, in BR orange/black lined locomotive green. As one of the last gestures, 10000/1 worked in multiple on the Royal Scot in March 1958.

In 1958 BR issued availability figures for the period 1 January-30 September 1957:

Fig 6: Diagram of SR 2000bhp locomotive No 10203 built at Brighton works in 1954. *(Author's collection)*

Locomotive Class	Days in Works	Days on Shed	Days Worked	Mileage
10000	70	43	148	80,636
10001	76	48	155	83,861
10201	62	30	181	104,532
10202	44	39	190	111,513
10203	84	35	153	74,865

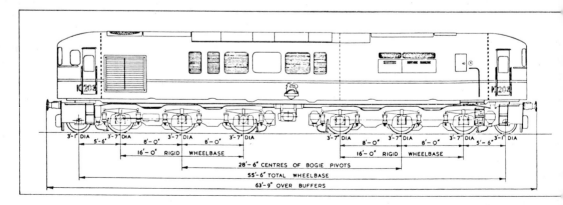

The down Royal Scot rumbles up Shap behind No 10203 on 13 July 1957. *(K. Hoole)*

They were not particularly startling figures, but comparison with some BR steam classes helps put them in perspective:

Locomotive Class	Days in Works	Days on Shed	Days Worked	Mileage
71000	24	58	148	39,709
Duchess	30	41	159	56,800
Britannia	30	42	160	43,158
Royal Scot	35	45	150	41,314
Jubilee	22	41	167	45,503

In October 1959 10203 was on Birmingham trains and recording some good performances with loads of up to nine coaches, running the 82.6 miles Rugby-Euston section in 68min giving an average start to stop speed of over 72mph, and a maximum of 95mph near Wembley. 1960-62 was a period in which the locomotives were employed mostly on Euston and Broad Street suburban duties, with odd forays to Rugby and Northampton; their visits to Derby works became prolonged and frequent, 10001 being the last to have a heavy overhaul, following a long stay in works.

The winter of 1962 saw 10201/3 arrive to stand forlornly in the works yard to be joined by 10000 and 10202 early in the new year. Withdrawal of these four took place in December 1963, but they were to remain until early 1968, when they were taken away to Cashmores, Great Bridge scrapyard. 10001, with a mileage of around one million, was withdrawn in March 1966, also being sold for scrap.

It was unfortunate that the preservation of diesels was not then in vogue, for one should have been kept for posterity. One recalls the abuse and ridicule hurled at these locomotives but there was no acknowledgement of the circumstances under which they had to operate, sharing maintenance and stabling with steam traction. Many times they had been seen in Willesden roundhouse on a Sunday evening lighting-up time wreathed in the sulphurous smoke of their companions, hardly fitting for such a sophisticated machine as a diesel-electric locomotive.

Their value as traffic machines was largely invalidated by their odd man out nature and they were thereby difficult to employ and maintain correctly; the latter was one reason for their frequent visits to works.

The majority of defects and problems centred on the control and ancillary equipment, and train-heating units, due in part to the use of unproven equipment, so far as British conditions were concerned, coupled with the lack of proper maintenance facilities. The main engines, generators, and traction motors performed remarkably well in the conditions under which they worked.

The experience gained with these five locomotives was valuable in so much that it enabled a steam-bound rail system to see the value afforded by diesel-electric locomotion; no doubt, it contributed to the decision to apply new forms of traction which gave the impetus to the 1955 BR modernisation programme.

TABLE 3
PROTOTYPE LMS AND SR/BR 1600-2000BHP DIESEL—ELECTRIC LOCOMOTIVES, 1947-1954

Locomotive Number	Wheel Arrangement	Builder	Order No	Date to Traffic	Date withdrawn from Service
10000	Co-Co	Derby	2510	11/47	12/63
10001	Co-Co	Derby	2510	7/48	3/66
10201	1Co-Co1	Ashford	3441	11/50	12/63
10202	1Co-Co1	Ashford	3441	8/51	12/63
10203	1Co-Co1	Brighton	3441	4/54	12/63

TABLE 4
MAIN DETAILS OF LOCOMOTIVES 10201/2 AND 10203

Description	10201/2	10203
Axle layout	1Co-Co1	1Co-Co1
Engine model	16SVT	16SVT Mk II
Engine rating	1750BHP at 850rpm	2000BHP at 850rpm
Locomotive weight, in working order	135 tons 0cwt	132 tons 16cwt
Brakes, locomotive	Straight air	Straight air
Brakes, train	Vacuum	Vacuum
Train heating	Spanner boiler	BR-Laidlaw Drew boiler
Boiler water tank capacity	880gals	840gals
Length over buffers	63ft 9in	63ft 9in
Overall width	9ft 3in	9ft 3in
Overall height	13ft 1in	13ft 1in
Wheel diameter, driving	3ft 7in	3ft 7in
Wheel diameter, guiding	3ft 1in	3ft 1in
Bogie pivots	28ft 6in	28ft 6in
Bogie wheelbase, rigid	16ft 0in	16ft 0in
Bogie wheelbase, total	21ft 6in	21ft 6in
Total wheelbase	55ft 6in	55ft 6in
Maximum speed	90mph	90mph
Maximum tractive	31,200 lb, later 48,000 lb	50,000 lb
Continuous tractive	14,000 lb, later 21,700 at 24.5 mph	30,000 lb at 19.5mph
Locomotive and boiler fuel capacity	1150gals	1180gals

CHAPTER 5

THE PROTOTYPE DELTIC LOCOMOTIVE

The desire to prove in traction service the unconventional Napier-Deltic opposed piston engine led, in 1955, to the construction of the most remarkable main line diesel-electric locomotive in the world. It was the initiative and tenacity of Lord Nelson of Stafford which persuaded the English Electric board to make use of the Deltic engine, not without considerable opposition from the EE Traction Division.

The limitation on many railway systems to speeding up their services, increasing traffic, and reducing expenses, was the fact that their tracks would not carry heavier and heavier locomotives with increasing power. The only solution was to use locomotives with extra axles to spread the weight, and usually this meant adding non-motored axles with the additional disadvantage of lowering adhesive weight. The adoption of diesel-hydraulic locomotives, at that time in increasing popularity because of their lighter weight, mainly attributable to their smaller and lighter high-speed diesel engines, and thus lighter mechanical portions, was one answer, but one which did not become universally popular.

English Electric, therefore, set about a locomotive with diesel-electric propulsion which would be light in weight, high in power, and with total adhesion, all axles being powered. At that time conventional diesel-electrics were equipped with engines running at 600-1000rpm. The weight of the engine and generator set was dependent on speed, for the use of high-speed engines can increase the power provided, within a locomotive of specified weight, while lighter engines meant a lighter mechanical portion, too.

The Deltic locomotive was designed to work fast passenger and freight work, and appeared as a 106 ton service weight unit of 3300bhp with a ratio of 72 lb per bhp. With its bright blue and yellow livery the Deltic caused a stir wherever it appeared.

The locomotive superstructure had a long equipment compartment, with driving cabs and long nose compartments at each end. The central section accommodated the two power units, arranged on each side of the centrally placed train-heating boiler unit. The batteries, principally for engine starting, were also accommodated between the power units on each side of the locomotive. Control cubicles at each end of the engine compartment formed the rear bulkheads of the cabs. The nose units had compartments containing air compressor, vacuum exhauster and traction motor blowers, resistances, brake equipment, main air reservoirs, auxiliary generator controls, and additional control equipment.

The roof over the equipment had removable sections, as had the nose ends. The generator roofs had the main air intakes for cooling the generators, and the roofs above the engines accommodated the radiators and fans, two for each engine, mechanically-driven by cardan shafts from their respective engines. The roof over the boiler, which also covered the silencers, accommodated the air intakes for the engines and boiler.

Fuel tanks and boiler feed water tanks were on the underframe between the bogies. The locomotive underframe and superstructure were fabricated complete as one unit, careful design and the use of light alloy keeping weight to a minimum. The four main longitudinals extended the full length of the underframe, the inner pair being fabricated flanged girders swept upwards over the bogies, the outer ones being rolled steel channels. Ample cross-members joined the longitudinals with reinforcement at the buffer beams.

The underframe was plated on the top surface and set down to form wells below the power units, the plating being welded and oil-tight to prevent leakage of oil spillage to the under gear. Drains were provided in the wells. The four fuel and two boiler-feed-water tanks, suspended on flexible mountings, were of light alloy. Fuel was filtered prior to entering the tanks, and between the interconnected tanks and the engines. The water tanks were insulated and steam heated against freezing, being fillable by hose or water column or by scoop from water troughs while running.

The superstructure was fabricated from rolled-steel sections with panels attached by arc-welding. The roof sections, doors, louvres, tread plates, much ducting and pipework, were of alloys. The body interior was insulated against sound and heat and lined with light alloy sheeting. Louvred intakes with filters were provided in the body sides and roof for the combustion air and cooling air. Each cab had two entrance doors, with access doors each side of a centrally-mounted control cubicle to the gangways through the power compartment. Two seats were provided, the driver being on the left.

Controls consisted of: master controller, train vacuum brake valve to the driver's right, and locomotive air brake to the left, and the instrument panel and indicator lights on the facing bulkhead. The master controller set all power circuits and controlled power to the road wheels. It had two operating handles: a master switch handle with four positions—off, forward, engine only, and reverse—and a control handle.

The latter had two positions, off and I. The power circuits were made at notch I, and further movement gave notchless control. Both controllers were lockable.

Protective equipment for wheel slip, engine oil pressure/coolant water temperature, loss of engine speed, power circuit protection, and fire were provided. Provision for isolation of individual traction motors and generator cut-out switching was made.

The bogies were of equalised type with swing bolsters, the load being carried on four side-bearers on each bolster and transmitted through double-elliptic laminated springs to spring planks suspended by long swing-links from the bogie frame. Equalising beams underslung from the axleboxes then distributed the load via four sets of helical springs. Bogie frames were

Fig 7: Diagram of the, then, world's most powerful single-unit diesel-electric locomotive, the prototype *Deltic* of 1955. This 3300bhp Co-Co unit was built at Preston in the old Dick, Kerr Works. Key: 1 Diesel engine; 2 Main generator; 3 Auxiliary generator; 4 Traction motor; 5 Traction-motor blower; 6 Control cubicle; 7 Heating boiler; 8 Battery; 9 Radiator; 10 Air compressor; 11 Exhauster; 12 Silencer; 13 Water tank; 14 Water pick-up; 15 Fuel tank; 16 Fuel pump; 17 Air-brake equipment; 18 Air reservoir; 19 Air-brake valve; 20 Hand brake; 21 Controller; 22 Driver's seat; 23 Assistant's seat. *(Author's collection)*

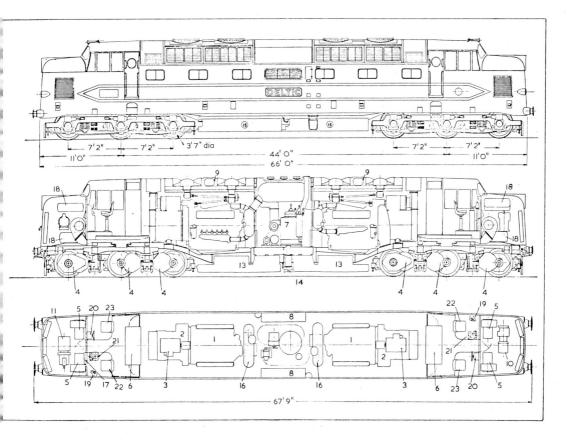

fabricated with box section side members with the transoms and headstocks riveted on, with gusset reinforcement to them. Hollow members provided, in part, the passage for traction motor blowing air. Timken roller bearing axleboxes were fitted.

The engines were Napier-Deltic opposed-piston units of type 18.25B with three banks totalling 18 cylinders giving 1650bhp each at 1500rpm. Electrical equipment comprised two main generators of English Electric type 831A with six-poles and a continuous rating of 1100kW at 1500rpm, and maximum current of 3000amp. The generators were connected to their respective engines by a flanged adaptor ring; drive from the engine was from the output shaft of the phasing gears from the three crankshafts.

A top-mounted 45kW auxiliary generator, gear driven from the phasing gears, was fitted. Both main generators were connected in series. Six EE type 526/A nose-suspended, axle-hung, force-ventilated traction motors with continuous ratings of 400hp, 533amp, 600V were connected in three series pairs in parallel across the main supply, driving the wheels through single reduction gearing of 59:21.

All the auxiliaries were driven electrically and comprised a motor driven compressor in No 1 nose unit supplying air for the locomotive brakes, sanders, control gear, warning horns; a vacuum exhauster driven by a two-speed rotary exhauster mounted in No 2 nose, for train braking; two traction motor blowers, one in each nose, drawing in air through nose-side filters, and supplying blowing air to the nearest bogie; and various small motors for fuel pumps, torque regulators, boiler auxiliaries, and cab heater fans. A Vapor-Clarkson train-heating boiler with an output of 2000lb was fitted.

The *Deltic* carrying its name in large letters on the body side panels, entered service on the LMR during October 1955 and was employed mostly on fast freights between Liverpool and London at night, working from Speke Junction shed. Although it continued to be so used until August 1956, it put in odd appearances on passenger work, its first apparently being the 10.10 Liverpool Lime Street-Euston train, the Merseyside Express, returning with the down Shamrock on 13 December 1955. This was a regular Edge Hill Pacific job.

On 16 August 1956 the locomotive ran from Crewe to Carlisle Durran Hill shed with the Mobile Testing Unit with a limited speed of 50mph, being due to start trials on the Settle-Carlisle line on Monday 20 August, which lasted into September. Coupled to a dynamometer car, and with up to three mobile test units to provide simulated loads coupled behind, the locomotive came through the trials with complete success; a full description was later published in the BR Locomotive Testing Bulletin No 19. Its performance conformed very closely to its 3300bhp rating, at 3250bhp. During the tests a maximum tractive effort of 45,550 lb was reached and held without wheel-slip for 2min.

With both engines working, 3250bhp was achieved and a continuous rail horse-power of 2650 recorded. This difference was due to the power needed to drive auxiliaries, main generator, and traction motors. At 40mph the *Deltic* gave 2410hp at the drawbar.

Among other trials, it is worthwhile recording that a 20 coach train of 642 tons, including dynamometer car, was hauled between Durran Hill, Carlisle, and Hellifield; this 82½ miles route includes the 1167ft altitude at Ais Gill. At the start the *Deltic* attained 46mph on the 1 in 133 from Durran Hill, then went on to the 1 in

eft: The prototype *Deltic* approaches Preston from the Blackpool line while on trials on the LMR main line in 1956. *(GEC Traction Ltd)*

Right: The prototype *Deltic* on the ER, backs out of Kings Cross after working an up express in early 1959. *(an S. Carr)*

29 at Low House at 54mph, accelerating rapidly to 70mph on the drop to Armathwaite. The 1 in 220 to milepost 294¾ was climbed with a drop from 72 to 68mph, to be slowed to 15mph by a PW check at Lazonby. However, acceleration raised this to 52mph on the level by Salkeld and up the 1 in 150 to Langwathby. From here speeds varied in the 66-69mph range until another PW check brought speed down to 5mph near Long Meg due to mining subsidence. After passing Appleby, ½ mile before Ormside, there is a continuous 17½ miles climb mostly of 1 in 100, apart from about two miles slightly easier at 1 in 162-215 between Griseburn and Crosby Garret, a mile of level track beyond this point, and one mile at 1 in 302 past Mallerstang signal box. The climb was started at 72mph, speed falling to 57mph in the first 3½ miles, held on the 1 in 162, but increasing to 63mph on the level past Crosby Garret. The long stretch of 1 in 100 past Kirkby Stephen reduced speed to 48mph before Mallerstang box, but speed increased there to 54mph and Ais Gill Summit was passed at 47mph. The *Deltic* had brought its 642 ton load over the 47 miles from Durran Hill in just over 5min, despite the slowings. A drawbar pull of 5 and 5½ tons was recorded on easy stretches with a maximum of over 8 tons at Ais Gill summit. Drawbar hp from Durran Hill varied between 2000 and 2400, with an average of 2200.

With one engine only, on other tests, the *Deltic* was able to exert a drawbar hp of 1100 at 20mph and 1270 at 25mph, less than half the combined output of two engines, because of power being absorbed by engine resistance and auxiliaries and the friction of the locomotive as a whole which is constant whatever the available power which must be set against the output recorded.

The fuel consumption for the 165 mile round trip was recorded as 210gal, or 0.8mpg with two engines and an average speed of 56.2mph. The locomotive gave excellent proof of its capabilities, and was officially praised for its smooth riding, the only criticism being engine noise, especially when idling in a station.

Haulage charts made from the mobile test unit and dynamometer-car road tests revealed that the *Deltic* could, at full power, take a 500 ton passenger train up a 1 in 100 gradient at 50mph and up a 1 in 75, like Shap, at 41mph. On a 1 in 400 gradient, 80mph could easily be maintained.

From 29 October 1956 the *Deltic* started regular work on the up Merseyside Express and down Shamrock, daily except Sundays. From early 1957 it was regularly on Euston-Glasgow/Perth workings as far as Carlisle, and back with sleeping car trains at night, and also returned to the Liverpool-Euston run. In June these workings were altered to include a Euston-Crewe round trip as well, involving a daily mileage of about 700 miles. The LMR period of service always concentrated on the Liverpool-Euston workings, with frequent visits to works for attention and modification.

In January 1959 *Deltic* was transferred to the ER at Hornsey shed for trials on the GN line. Its main problem here was its restricted loading gauge which prohibited it from some platforms at Kings Cross. Its stay was soon halted by an engine failure necessitating a return to EE.

Its peregrinations took it to York for two days of trials in mid-January, during which it ran to Berwick with an inspection saloon on the 16th, proving out of gauge and succeeding in dislodging platform copings at Manors Station, and losing its cab footsteps at Darlington.

In March it took part in a test run between

Kings Cross and Grantham, turning on Barkston triangle. The tests were to check high speed braking potential and performance with a dynamometer car and nine coaches weighing 355 tons. Braking tests were made at 60, 90, and 102mph. The average speed recorded in the down direction between Tallington and Stoke summit was 88mph, with a peak of 92mph at Little Bytham and Corby Glen, the summit being surmounted at 85mph. A top speed of 106mph was achieved. A few days later on 9 March with a similar load, and on 11 March with 15 coaches, it ran between Kings Cross and Leeds. A week later it took a test train from Kings Cross to Newcastle, and was soon working on odd occasions the 08.20 over the same route. Mineral train trials, with 50 loaded vacuum brake-fitted wagons, dynamometer car, and brake van were undertaken between London and Doncaster the same month.

Its first visit to Scotland proper was to Edinburgh on 8 June 1959 via the Waverley route. While at Edinburgh it worked round trips daily from Craigentinny to Berwick via the outer circle suburban line and Waverley station, returning via the inner circle. Loads of up to 18 coaches with the Hallade track recording coach were hauled with complete success. The trials ceased on 12 June.

On 22 June it commenced regular Monday to Friday work on Kings Cross main line trains such as the White Rose to Leeds; Leeds-Doncaster; returning to London with a Hull train from Doncaster. The locomotive returned north with the 20.20 to Edinburgh as far as Doncaster, followed by another southward run back to London on a parcels train. On Saturdays it was on such Kings Cross jobs as the 08.18 to Doncaster returning on the 13.42 Filey-Kings Cross from Doncaster. It was still prohibited from regular duties over the NER.

The Deltic returned to VF in July 1959, reappearing on the White Rose repainted and overhauled on 27 August. At the turn of 1960 it was in Stratford works and during 1960 was mostly on GN line workings, interspaced with further high-speed test runs between Kings Cross and Grantham.

Deltic's end came in March 1961, following its failure on a Doncaster turn, going to Vulcan Foundry, from which it was not to reappear until 1963, when it was presented to the Science Museum in London, moving there, its last journey being by road, on 28 April 1963. It covered over 450,000 miles on BR between 1955

and 1961, of which about 200,000 miles were undertaken on the LMR.

Operating experience with the prototype Deltic made it clear to Mr G. F. Fiennes of the ER Board that a feasible production locomotive could be produced to undertake the most onerous duties on BR. During its relatively short life a number of modifications were carried out, the more important including alterations made to enable the locomotive to operate on lightly-loaded or slower services with only one engine running. This involved major attention to enable a single engine to drive all six traction motors. The wheel treads had given trouble with shelling, and shock absorbers to improve riding in the 12-52mph range were fitted. It was originally built for a maximum of 90mph but this soon proved too low for a locomotive of such power, and gear ratios were altered to give 106mph. It suffered attacks of the perennial disease of train heating boiler trouble in common with other BR diesels.

It was officially recorded that the diesel engines required little routine maintenance and proved remarkably free of trouble for a first traction application, although a certain amount of engine changing was carried out. Throughout its BR running Deltic was under the constant eye of English Electric and Napier technicians. Quite extraordinary haulage and acceleration capacity relative to other British locomotives was obtained, because even with 500 tons tail load over 5bhp per ton was available. However, that said, the Deltic was not really stretched by BR running of the period of its trials. The locomotive carried English Electric works No 2007 of 1955.

TABLE 5

MAIN DETAILS AND DIMENSIONS OF THE PROTOTYPE DELTIC LOCOMOTIVE

Description	Data
Axle layout	Co-Co
Engine model	Two engines D18-25
Engine rating	1650BHP at 1500rpm each
Locomotive weight, in working order	106 tons 0cwt
Brakes, locomotive	Air
Brakes, train	Vacuum
Train heating	Vapor-Clarkson boiler
Boiler water tank capacity	600gals
Length over buffers	67ft 9in
Overall width	8ft 9½in
Overall height	12ft 10in
Wheel diameter	3ft 7in
Bogie pivots	44ft 0in
Bogie wheelbase	14ft 4in
Total wheelbase	58ft 4in
Maximum speed	106mph
Maximum tractive effort	52,500 lb
Continuous tractive effort	29,000 lb at 35mph
Locomotive and boiler fuel capacity	800gals

CHAPTER 6

BR D8000 CLASS: THE STANDARD TYPE 1

November 1955 saw the long-awaited announcement that BR was ordering £10,000,000 worth of main line diesel locomotives. A total of 171 were authorised of 13 different types as a pilot scheme under which trials would be made before placing further orders under the £1250,000,000 15-year modernisation and re-equipment programme envisaging the provision of up to 2,500 line-service diesel locomotives, in addition to shunters and railcars.

Three general categories were included in the first orders:

Type A 800-1000bhp
Type B 1000-1250bhp
Type C 2000-2300bhp

141 locomotives were ordered from the British locomotive industry, and 30 from BR workshops. The largest of the former orders went to English Electric, for 40 diesel-electric locomotives of three types as set out below:

No of Loco	BHP	Wheel Arrangement	Engine Make	Engine Type	Transmission Make	Reg. Allocation
10	2000	1Co-Co1	EE	16SVT	EE	ER
10	1100	Bo-Bo	Napier	Deltic	EE	ER
20	1000	Bo-Bo	EE	8SVT	EE	LMR

Shortly after the above details were released, a further three locomotives of Type C were added, making 174 locomotives in all, and adding three more to the total to be built at BR workshops.

The honour of delivering the first of the locomotives of the pilot scheme went to the English Electric Co, Ltd, whose Vulcan Foundry put in hand the batch of 20 1000bhp Bo-Bo diesel-electrics to be numbered D8000-19 for service on the LMR. The D8000 Class are mainly intended for freight work, and for this reason are of the hood type with a single cab at one end, and did not have any train-heating equipment. They are, of course, quite suitable for passenger haulage and during summer months have proved this.

The underframe is based on four channel-section longitudinals divided into pairs, each pair being joined at the top and bottom by plating to form box sections. They are strongly cross-membered at intervals by welded transoms. The centre parts of the box sections are sealed to form two fuel tanks connected together by two of the transom members which act as balancing pipes. The drag boxes are welded at both ends of the underframe and carry standard buffing and drawgear. Provision is made for centre couplers although in nearly 20 years of operation they have not been fitted. The two underslung battery boxes between the bogies are well ventilated.

The superstructure is of the hood or bonnet type with a full-width driving cab at one end ostensibly regarded as the rear end like a steam locomotive cab. The cab has two seats and two side entrance doors. Forward vision is somewhat restricted by the engine bonnet, but rear visibility is excellent. Their use in service with cab leading is testimony of this. The cab is resiliently mounted on the underframe to reduce noise.

The engine bonnet has ample side-access doors and is built on a prefabricated frame fixed to the underframe by welding. Removable roof sections over the power equipment, control cubicle, and end compartment facilitate maintenance. In addition, hinged hatches over the cylinder heads permit piston withdrawal, and there is a removable hatch over the pressure-chargers.

The bogies have fabricated frames with welded box-section solebars and riveted transom and headstocks. The superstructure weight is transmitted to the bogies through a single bolster on each bogie, the bolster being carried on semi-elliptic laminated springs, carried on a swing plank supported from the bogie by inclined swing links. Springing between bogie frame and the wheels is by coil springs located between the underside of the bogie frame and the top side of the forged-steel equalising beams, which are underslung from the Timken roller-bearing axleboxes.

Braking control equipment is of Oerlikon type made by Davies and Metcalfe, each driving position having two brake handles, locomotive air brake and vacuum train brake; a proportional valve ensures equal applications of locomotive and train brake. A deadman's pedal is fitted at the driving position.

Most of the control gear is housed in the

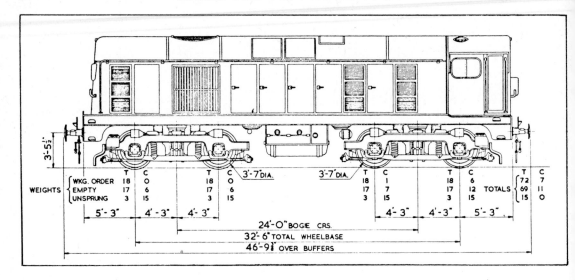

		T	C		T	C			T	C		T	C		T	C
WEIGHTS	WKG. ORDER	18	0		18	0	3'-7"DIA.	3'-7"DIA.	18	1		18	6		72	7
	EMPTY	17	6		17	6			17	7		17	12	TOTALS	69	11
	UNSPRUNG	3	15		3	15			3	15		3	15		15	0

5'-3"   4'-3"   4'-3"   4'-3"   4'-3"   5'-3"

24'-0" BOGIE CRS.
32'-6" TOTAL WHEELBASE
46'-9¾" OVER BUFFERS

single cubicle facing into the cab, and placed transversely across the locomotive. The rest of the control gear, including torque and voltage regulators, is placed behind the cubicle on a bridge support set at cantrail height across the interior of the engine casing.

The driver's controls are set in a desk and include a lockable master controller with two handles. Starting the locomotive is by moving one handle to the engine-only position and pressing the engine starting button. This motors the generator from the battery, turning the engine over until it fires. Once this has occurred the handle may be moved to select direction of travel, from which time the second handle, which controls the power output, is used. The usual warning and indicator lights are fitted, together with instrumentation.

An English Electric 8 SVT Mk II vee type engine, giving 1000bhp at 850rpm, is fitted. Two Napier exhaust-gas turbo-chargers are fitted at the driving end. At the free end is an extension of the crankshaft, providing a mechanical drive to the radiator fan. The main generator is bolted onto the engine, the whole unit being resiliently mounted.

Cooling of the engine oil and water is by a double bank Spiral Tube radiator, one radiator

panel being mounted at each side of the engine bonnet. The roof-mounted radiator fan draws air across the radiators and expels it through the roof. Radiator shutters, operable from the cab, were fitted. Air taken into the locomotive interior passes through oil-wetted filters.

The main generator, of type EE 819/3C, is a dc self-ventilated, single-bearing unit with a continuous rating of 1070amp at 600V. It is provided with both a separately-excited winding for normal running and a series winding for engine starting. The auxiliary generator, over-hung from the free end of the main generator, is maintained at a constant 110V and supplies power for battery charging, operating the control gear, driving the compressor motor, exhauster motor, and traction motor blowers.

Four EE type 526/5D nose-suspended traction motors drive the wheels via single-reduction spur gearing. They are series wound dc machines with field weakening and a continuous rating of 600amp at 300V. Force-ventilation is provided.

By the time the locomotives were under construction to the pilot orders, BR had revised its power classification from A, B, and C to:

Type 1 Line Service Locomotives,
  up to 1000bhp
Type 2 Line Service Locomotives,
  1000-1499bhp
Type 3 Line Service Locomotives,
  1500-1999bhp
Type 4 Line Service Locomotives,
  2000-2999bhp
Type 5 Line Service Locomotives,
  3000bhp upwards

The D8000 Class, now BR Class 20, were the first diesels of the modernisation programme to be delivered, the first Type 1, and as it has turned out, the last, or only Type 1 design to have survived in BR running stock.

They were built during the 1957-68 period to a

total of 228 units, construction taking place at VF, which built 135, and RSH, which construc-ted the remaining 93. Like the D200 Class, they have always been allocated to the LMR, ScR, and ER.

The LMR took the first 20, D8000-19, during 1957/8 which were allocated to the old North London shed, Devons Road, Bow, where, together with a few shunters and ten other Type 1 units of 800bhp, they replaced a horde of LMS 0-6-0Ts of Class 3F. This was the first BR depot to be dieselised for line and shunter duties. The locomotives were delivered following tests with each locomotive between Vulcan Foundry and Penrith, and were soon at work on London area freight services, although dispersal for trials and training at other sheds soon followed. Examples went to Willesden, Rugby, Crewe, and Toton, while D8006 was sent to Scotland in late 1958, in Fifeshire and on Deeside. The LMR ones were soon operating in multiple on West Coast freights between London and Crewe, while D8002 from Rugby spent some time on Northampton-Birmingham passenger trains in the summer of 1958, when the lack of train-heating was not noticeable.

This batch later found its way to the ER at Stratford, Sheffield, and Immingham, the Scottish sheds at Haymarket and Eastfield, and to the NER at Gateshead where they worked Northumberland coal traffic, York and Leeds. While at London area sheds they found their way to such South Coast resorts as Margate and Ramsgate on excursion traffic, in addition to Tilbury line services at weekends.

The second LMR batch, D8035-44, was officially intended for the GE section of the ER, and the first few started by being allocated to Norwich shed, but on loan to the LMR. They were sent new to Willesden and Devons Road, the ER receiving 10 800bhp units in exchange. Subsequently some were allocated to Camden Shed, where their use on empty carriage duties at Euston, a task of Willesden ones also, was common for a period. They found their way to Crewe, Toton, and Birmingham area depots, and to the ER at Tinsley.

The ER at Hornsey shed on the GN line took the batch D8020-7 in the autumn of 1959. They were used on Kings Cross empty carriage workings, but mostly were confined to Hitchin and Hatfield freight workings. The late spring of 1962 saw some on suburban passenger work out of Kings Cross, and even on Cambridge trains. The shortage of suitable power, because of

failings of the D5900s, had largely brought this situation, and unfortunately, it was continued at various times of pressure. The batch was moved to Finsbury Park when this new depot opened, but subsequently all moved north.

The largest ER batch, D8050-69, was delivered in the second quarter of 1961 to Tinsley depot where they were employed on Sheffield area freight duties, being outstationed at such other local sheds as Brightside, and working in the Worksop, Langwith, Shirebrook, Chesterfield areas. In the summer months they took their share in workings to the coast with Saturday passenger trains and excursion traffic.

In June 1965 D8069 was loaned to the WR at Cardiff Canton for a short trial period. At the same time Tinsley received additional locomotives and some were used at Lincoln shed where they performed banking work between Gunhouse Junction and Scunthorpe.

The Scottish Region's first batch, D8028-34 of December-March 1959/60, was initially alloca-

ted to Haymarket (Leith Central), Aberdeen and Inverness depots. In common with later examples built for service in Scotland, the cab sides had recesses for the fitting of token catching equipment for single track lines. Their duties took them over the Highland and GNSR routes.

The 1961/62 deliveries to Scotland comprised locomotives D8070-8127, all of which went to Glasgow at Eastfield and Polmadie where in conjunction with type 1 units of another make, they eliminated many steam freight workings and allowed full dieselisation of the duties of a number of smaller sheds. Of this batch D8085/6 were fitted with Westinghouse compressed air train braking equipment to enable them to haul electric multiple-units between Hyndland and Shields depots.

In the summer months the Scottish locomotives proved very popular on passenger duties and excursions at weekends, and even worked to Carlisle and Newcastle on relief

Nos D8061 and D8064 in multiple accelerate away from Scarborough with a weekend Saturday train for Sheffield on 13 June 1964. *(Norman Skinner)*

trains. Difficulties with new Glasgow suburban electric trains in the late summer of 1961 saw the D8000s on electric train duties, notably on the Helensburgh line. They are capable of good turns of speed and have covered the 47 mile Glasgow-Edinburgh run in 50min with passenger trains. In 1962 they were put on to Fifeshire coal train workings from Thornton Junction shed, while the summer again saw them on passenger work between Glasgow and St Andrews, with loads of up to 12 coaches.

Regular longer distance duties brought paired Eastfield units as far south as Coventry on the Linwood car components trains from April 1963, their layover period often being used by the LMR on Rugby-Coventry-Birmingham local trains.

With the delivery of D8127 in July 1962, BR had decided that the English Electric Type 1 would no longer figure in their future orders. Meanwhile BR standardised straight from the drawing board, a good-looking, twin-power-unit, centre-cab, 900bhp diesel-electric from another manufacturer, which was built to a total of 117 units between 1962 and 1965. They proved a costly experience for BR because all withdrawn by the end of 1971, after less than a 10 year life. The obvious unsuitability of these good-visibility units prompted a hurried return to the English Electric design and an enquiry for a further 50 materialised in practice as an additional 100 locomotives numbered D8128-99/8300-27, deliveries recommencing in January 1966.

The new batch differed from the previous 128 locomotives by the provision of four-digit nose and cab indicator boxes, and in various modifications of auxiliary gear. The 100 new units were allocated regionally as follows: D8128-33, ER at Tinsley; D8134-99, LMR, Birmingham area and Toton; D8300-15, NER, York and Thornaby; D8316-27, Scotland, Haymarket and Polmadie.

The most interesting developments with these

Nos D8310 and D8315 with four-digit indicator boxes, head an up freight over the old NER main line at Penshaw North in thunder and rain on 18 August 1967. *(Ian S. Carr).*

later D8000s was the fitting of some with slow-speed-control. D8179 of the LMR and D8317, a Scottish example, were involved in extensive trials in mid-1967 on the Wirksworth branch with a load of 1260 tons, followed by half this load and one locomotive. The slow-speed-control was designed to permit the non-stop slow speed loading/unloading of what became known as merry-go-round freight trains, used largely to carry coal from collieries to power stations. On the LMR the new locomotives were covering many Midland freight duties, including through workings to Immingham and Lincoln.

New deliveries to Scotland permitted further dieselisation in Ayrshire, and of banking on Beattock bank from May 1966. D8317-27 were fitted with slow-speed-control, but deliveries were also slow between November 1967 and February 1968.

In the first quarter of 1969, tests of trackside equipment in Scotland were carried out before merry-go-round coal trains serving Longannet power station with thirty-six hopper-wagons were introduced from mid-summer. On Clydeside the Scottish steel complexes were being served by regularly timetabled iron-ore trains between the Clyde ore-terminal on a merry-go-round basis, again D8000-hauled. In the North East, York used D8300-9 on local freights, with odd runs on York-Hull via Selby expresses, while the Tees-side ones were employed on Tees yard freight duties.

As part of the general programme to obtain maximum use of locomotives, long through workings were evolved which took locomotives away from their parent depot for days at a time. As a result LMR examples from Toton depot

TABLE 6
MAIN DETAILS AND DIMENSIONS OF D8000 CLASS NOW CLASS 20

Details	Data
Axle layout	Bo-Bo
Engine model	8SVT Mk II
Engine rating	1000bhp at 850 rpm
Length over buffers	46ft 9 3/8in
Overall width	8ft 9in
Overall height	12ft 7 3/8in
Wheel diameter	3ft 7in
Bogie pivots	24ft 0in
Bogie wheelbase	8ft 6in
Total wheelbase	32ft 6in
Maximum speed	75 mph
Maximum tractive effort	42,200 lb at 26% adhesion
Continuous tractive effort	25,000 lb at 11 mph
Continuous rail hp	770
Locomotive fuel capacity	380/400 gals
Weight in working order depending on variations in installed equipment	71 tons 19 cwt to 72 tons 14 cwt

took freights to Tees-side from late 1972, and other duties later saw them working to Severn Tunnel Junction WR, again in multiple. Scottish units meanwhile were employed on 840 ton merry-go-round trains from Cowdenbeath opencast coal sites to Longannet.

Braking modifications and equipment variations in Class 20 locomotives have caused weight differences, so that locomotives with air brake and train vacuum brake weigh variously in working order/empty: 71 tons 19 cwt/69 tons 3 cwt; 72 tons 1 cwt/69 tons 5 cwt, and 72 tons 14 cwt/69 tons 18 cwt. However the fitting of locomotive straight air/automatic air brakes, and automatic air/air-continuous vacuum for the train has produced further variations of 72 tons 5 cwt/69 tons 6 cwt; 72 tons 6 cwt/70 tons 10 cwt and 72 tons 7 cwt/69 tons 11 cwt.

Allocations by the autumn of 1975 was basically to five depots, Toton on the LMR, Tinsley and Immingham on the ER, and Eastfield and Haymarket in Scotland. The BR economy measures at the time of going to press have resulted in five of Toton's locomotives going into store, officially at Derby, but some were soon receiving attention in Crewe works, so all the class were still in stock. The Class 20 locomotives have achieved a figure of 90 per cent availability, and are well ahead of any other BR diesel type in this respect.

Table 7   D8000 CLASS TYPE 1 – LATER BR CLASS 20

Original BR No	Works No VF or RSH	Works No Eng Elec	Date to Traffic	Reg New	Allocation Sep'75
D8000	VF D375	2347	P7/57	LM	LM
D8001	VF D376	2348	P7/57	LM	LM
D8002	VF D377	2349	P8/57	LM	SC
D8003	VF D378	2350	P9/57	LM	E
D8004	VF D379	2351	P8/57	LM	LM
D8005	VF D380	2352	P10/57	LM	LM
D8006	VF D381	2353	P10/57	LM	LM
D8007	VF D382	2354	P10/57	LM	E
D8008	VF D383	2355	P10/57	LM	LM
D8009	VF D384	2356	P11/57	LM	LM
D8010	VF D385	2357	P11/57	LM	E
D8011	VF D386	2358	P11/57	LM	SC
D8012	VF D 387	2359	P12/57	LM	LM
D8013	VF D388	2360	P12/57	LM	LM
D8014	VF D389	2361	P12/57	LM	LM
D8015	VF D390	2362	P13/57	LM	SC
D8016	VF D391	2363	P1/58	LM	LM
D8017	VF D392	2364	P1/58	LM	SC
D8018	VF D393	2365	P2/58	LM	LM
D8019	VF D394	2366	P3/58	LM	SC
D8020	RSH 8052	2742	10/59	E	E
D8021	RSH 8053	2743	10/59	E	E
D8022	RSH 8054	2744	10/59	E	E
D8023	RSH 8055	2745	11/59	E	E
D8024	RSH 8056	2746	11/59	E	SC
D8025	RSH 8057	2747	11/59	E	E
D8026	RSH 8058	2748	12/59	E	E
D8027	RSH 8059	2749	12/59	E	SC
D8028	RSH 8060	2750	P13/59	SC	E
D8029	RSH 8061	2751	P13/59	SC	E
D8030	RSH 8062	2752	P13/59	SC	SC
D8031	RSH 8063	2753	P1/60	SC	E
D8032	RSH 8064	2754	P1/60	SC	E
D8033	RSH 8065	2755	P2/60	SC	E
D8034	RSH 8066	2756	P3/60	SC!	SC
D8035	VF D482	2757	P9/59	LM	LM
D8036	VF D483	2758	P10/59	LM	SC
D8037	VF D484	2759	P10/59	LM	LM
D8038	VF D485	2760	P10/59	LM	LM
D8039	VF D486	2761	P10/59	LM	SC
D8040	VF D487	2762	P10/59	LM	LM
D8041	VF D488	2763	P11/59	LM	LM
D8042	VF D489	2764	P11/59	LM	LM
D8043	VF D490	2765	P11/59	LM	LM
D8044	VF D491	2766	P11/59	LM	LM
D8045	VF D492	2767	12/59	E	LM
D8046	VF D493	2768	12/59	E	SC
D8047	VF D494	2769	12/59	E	LM
D8048	VF D495	2770	12/59	E	SC
D8049	VF D496	2771	12/59	E	E
D8050	RSH 8208	2956	3/61	E	E
D8051	RSH 8209	2957	3/61	E	E
D8052	RSH 8210	2958	3/61	E	E
D8053	RSH 8211	2959	4/61	E	E
D8054	RSH 8212	2960	6/61	E	E
D8055	RSH 8213	2961	4/61	E	SC
D8056	RSH 8214	2962	4/61	E	E
D8057	RSH 8215	2963	5/61	E	E
D8058	RSH 8216	2964	5/61	E	E
D8059	RSH 8217	2965	5/61	E	E
D8060	RSH 8218	2966	5/61	E	E
D8061	RSH 8219	2967	5/61	E	E
D8062	RSH 8220	2968	5/61	E	LM
D8063	RSH 8221	2969	6/61	E	LM
D8064	RSH 8222	2970	6/61	E	LM
D8065	RSH 8223	2971	6/61	E	LM
D8066	RSH 8224	2972	6/61	E	LM
D8067	RSH 8225	2973	6/61	E	LM
D8068	RSH 8226	2974	6/61	E	LM
D8069	RSH 8227	2975	6/61	E	LM
D8070	RSH 8228	2976	P7/61	SC	LM
D8071	RSH 8229	2977	P7/61	SC	LM
D8072	RSH 8230	2978	P7/61	SC	LM
D8073	RSH 8231	2979	P8/61	SC	LM
D8074	RSH 8232	2980	P8/61	SC	LM
D8075	RSH 8233	2981	P8/61	SC	LM
D8076	RSH 8234	2982	P8/61	SC	LM
D8077	RSH 8235	2983	P8/61	SC	LM
D8078	RSH 8236	2984	P8/61	SC	SC
D8079	RSH 8237	2985	P9/61	SC	SC
D8080	RSH 8238	2986	P9/61	SC	SC
D8081	RSH 8239	2987	P9/61	SC	LM
D8082	RSH 8240	2988	P9/61	SC	LM
D8083	RSH 8241	2989	P10/61	SC	SC
D8084	RSH 8242	2990	P10/61	SC	LM
D8085	RSH 8243	2991	P10/61	SC	SC
D8086	RSH 8244	2992	P10/61	SC	SC
D8087	RSH 8245	2993	P10/61	SC	LM
D8088	RSH 8246	2994	P10/61	SC	LM
D8089	RSH 8247	2995	P10/61	SC	SC
D8090	RSH 8248	2996	P10/61	SC	LM
D8091	RSH 8249	2997	P11/61	SC	E
D8092	RSH 8250	2998	P11/61	SC	E
D8093	RSH 8251	2999	P11/61	SC	SC

Table 7 Cont.   D8000 Class Type 1 — Later BR Class 20

Original BR No	Works No VF or RSH	Works No Eng Elec	Date to Traffic	Reg New	Allocation Sep '75
D8094	RSH 8252	3000	P11/61	SC	SC
D8095	RSH 8253	3001	P11/61	SC	SC
D8096	RSH 8254	3002	P11/61	SC	SC
D8097	RSH 8256	3004	P12/61	SC	LM
D8098	RSH 8255	3003	P12/61	SC	SC
D8099	RSH 8257	3005	P12/61	SC	SC
D8100	RSH 8258	3006	P12/61	SC	SC
D8101	RSH 8259	3007	P12/61	SC	SC
D8102	RSH 8260	3008	P12/61	SC	SC
D8103	RSH 8261	3009	P12/61	SC	SC
D8104	RSH 8262	3010	P13/61	SC	SC
D8105	RSH 8263	3011	P13/61	SC	SC
D8106	RSH 8264	3012	P13/61	SC	SC
D8107	RSH 8265	3013	P13/61	SC	SC
D8108	RSH 8266	3014	P13/61	SC	SC
D8109	RSH 8267	3015	P12/61	SC	SC
D8110	RSH 8268	3016	P1/62	SC	SC
D8111	RSH 8269	3017	P1/62	SC	SC
D8112	RSH 8270	3018	P1/62	SC	SC
D8113	RSH 8271	3019	P2/62	SC	LM
D8114	RSH 8272	3020	P2/62	SC	SC
D8115	RSH 8273	3021	P2/62	SC	SC
D8116	RSH 8274	3022	P2/62	SC	SC
D8117	RSH 8275	3023	P2/62	SC	SC
D8118	RSH 8276	3024	P3/62	SC	SC
D8119	RSH 8277	3025	P3/62	SC	E
D8120	RSH 8278	3026	P3/62	SC	SC
D8121	RSH 8279	3027	P3/62	SC	SC
D8122	RSH 8280	3028	P3/62	SC	SC
D8123	RSH 8281	3029	P4/62	SC	SC
D8124	RSH 8282	3030	P4/62	SC	SC
D8125	RSH 8283	3031	P5/62	SC	SC
D8126	RSH 8284	3032	P5/62	SC	SC
D8127	RSH 8285	3033	P8/62	SC	E
D8128	VF D998	3599	1/66	E	E
D8129	VF D999	3600	2/66	E	E
D8130	VF D1000	3601	2/66	E	E
D8131	VF D1001	3602	2/66	E	E
D8132	VF D1002	3603	3/66	E	E
D8133	VF D1003	3604	3/66	E	E
D8134	VF D1004	3605	P3/66	LM	LM
D8135	VF D1005	3606	P3/66	LM	LM
D8136	VF D1006	3607	P4/66	LM	LM
D8137	VF D1007	3608	P4/66	LM	SC
D8138	VF D1008	3609	P4/66	LM	SC
D8139	VF D1009	3610	P5/66	LM	LM
D8140	VF D1010	3611	P5/66	LM	LM
D8141	VF D1011	3612	P5/66	LM	LM
D8142	VF D1013	3614	P5/66	LM	LM
D8143	VF D1012	3613	P7/66	LM	LM
D8144	VF D1014	3615	P7/66	LM	E
D8145	VF D1015	3616	P6/66	LM	E
D8146	VF D1016	3617	P6/66	LM	LM
D8147	VF D1017	3618	P7/66	LM	LM
D8148	VF D1018	3619	P7/66	LM	LM
D8149	VF D1019	3620	P7/66	LM	LM
D8150	VF D1020	3621	P7/66	LM	LM
D8151	VF D1021	3622	P7/66	LM	LM
D8152	VF D1022	3623	P8/66	LM	LM
D8153	VF D1023	3624	P8/66	LM	LM
D8154	VF D1024	3625	P8/66	LM	LM
D8155	VF D1025	3626	P8/66	LM	LM
D8156	VF D1026	3627	P8/66	LM	LM
D8157	VF D1027	3628	P8/66	LM	LM
D8158	VF D1028	3629	P8/66	LM	LM
D8159	VF D1029	3630	P9/66	LM	LM
D8160	VF D1030	3631	P12/66	LM	LM
D8161	VF D1031	3632	P10/66	LM	LM
D8162	VF D1032	3633	P10/66	LM	LM
D8163	VF D1033	3634	P10/66	LM	LM
D8164	VF D1034	3635	P10/66	LM	LM
D8165	VF D1035	3636	P10/66	LM	LM
D8166	VF D1036	3637	P11/66	LM	LM
D8167	VF D1037	3638	P11/66	LM	LM
D8168	VF D1038	3639	P11/66	LM	LM
D8169	VF D1039	3640	P11/66	LM	LM
D8170	VF D 1040	3641	P11/66	LM	LM
D8171	VF D1041	3642	P11/66	LM	LM
D8172	VF D1042	3643	P11/66	LM	LM
D8173	VF D1043	3644	P12/66	LM	LM
D8174	VF D1044	3645	P11/66	LM	LM
D8175	VF D1045	3646	P12/66	LM	LM
D8176	VF D1046	3647	P12/66	LM	LM
D8177	VF D1047	3648	P12/66	LM	LM
D8178	VF D1054	3659	P13/66	LM	LM
D8179	VF D1055	3660	P13/66	LM	SC
D8180	VF D1056	3661	P13/66	LM	LM
D8181	VF D1057	3662	P13/66	LM	LM
D8182	VF D1058	3663	P13/66	LM	LM
D8183	VF D1059	3664	P13/66	LM	LM
D8184	VF D1060	3665	P13/66	LM	SC
D8185	VF D1061	3666	P2/67	LM	LM
D8186	VF D1062	3667	P1/67	LM	LM
D8187	VF D1063	3668	P1/67	LM	LM
D8188	VF D1064	3669	P1/67	LM	LM
D8189	VF D1065	3670	P1/67	LM	LM
D8190	VF D1066	3671	P1/67	LM	LM
D8191	VF D1067	3672	P2/67	LM	SC
D8192	VF D1068	3673	P2/67	LM	LM
D8193	VF D1069	3674	P2/67	LM	LM
D8194	VF D1070	3675	P2/67	LM	LM
D8195	VF D1071	3676	P2/67	LM	LM
D8196	VF D1072	3677	P2/67	LM	LM
D8197	VF D1073	3678	P2/67	LM	LM
D8198	VF D1074	3679	P4/67	LM	LM
D8199	VF D1075	3680	P4/67	LM	LM
D8300	VF D1076	3681	3/67	E	E
D8301	VF D1077	3682	3/67	E	E
D8302	VF—————	———	3/67	E	E
D8303	VF D1079	3684	3/67	E	E
D8304	VF —————	———	3/67	E	E
D8305	VF D1081	3686	3/67	E	E
D8306	VF D1082	3687	4/67	E	E
D8307	VF D1083	3688	4/67	E	E
D8308	VF D1084	3689	4/67	E	E
D8309	VF D1085	3690	4/67	E	E
D8310	VF D1086	3691	4/67	E	E
D8311	VF D1087	3692	4/67	E	E
D8312	VF D1088	3693	4/67	E	E
D8313	VF D1089	3694	5/67	E	E
D8314	VF D1090	3695	5/67	E	E
D8315	VF D1091	3696	5/67	E	E
D8316	VF D1092	3697	P6/67	SC	SC
D8317	VF D1093	3698	11/67	SC	SC
D8318	VF D1094	3699	11/67	SC	SC
D8319	VF D1095	3700	1/68	SC	SC
D8320	VF D1096	3701	11/67	SC	SC
D8321	VF D1097	3702	12/67	SC	SC
D8322	VF D1098	3703	12/67	SC	SC
D8323	VF D1099	3704	10/67	SC	SC
D8324	VF D1100	3705	11/67	SC	SC
D8325	VF D1101	3706	11/67	SC	SC
D8326	VF D1078	3683	2/68	SC	SC
D8327	VF D1080	3685	2/68	SC	SC

Locomotives D8302/4 carry no maker's works numbers.

CHAPTER 7

THE 2000BHP D200s: BACKBONE OF BR (CLASS 40)

The delivery of the first large diesel-electric locomotive to BR took place in April 1958 when D200, the first of ten 2000bhp English Electric locomotives ordered in 1955, was placed in service on the Eastern Region. Built at Vulcan Foundry, they are eight axle units of 18 tons maximum axle-loading, designed for mixed traffic work with a service weight of 133 tons.

The design bears a strong family resemblance

to 10203 which, we have seen, was built in 1954 as the third of a prototype batch ordered by the SR in 1946, and also to a 2000bhp type built by English Electric for Rhodesia. The mechanical design is typical of the maker's practice, at that time comprising a full-width superstructure with a cab and nose unit at each end.

The superstructure has six compartments: two nose units, two cabs, engine room, and

Scottish based class 40 No 262, with nose end doors removed and four-digit indicator fitted, passes Low Gill, south of Tebay, with an up express on 17 July 1971. (G. T. Heavyside)

with hoses. The boiler in the first batch was a Stone-Vapor unit with an output of 2700 lb per hour.

The bogies are heavy 1Co type, very similar to those used on locomotives 10201-10203, being side plate frame units with rigid cross stretchers riveted in. The middle stretchers carry the four segmental pivot bearings. The dragbox is built into the bogie frame and carries two spring-loaded side bearers. Standard buffing and drawgear are fitted.

The outer axle of each bogie is a pony truck with short control links carried ahead of the axle and anchored to the buffer beam. All axleboxes have Timken taper roller bearings with a cannon type box on the pony trucks. Springing is applied directly to the axleboxes and consists of a pair of reverse-camber laminated springs to each motored axle with auxiliary coil springs on each link.

Braking on the locomotive is by compressed air from a Westinghouse cylinder, operated by a handle in each cab for the locomotive only; a second handle applies the train vacuum brakes and the locomotive air brakes proportionally. A hand brake and deadman's pedal is fitted in each cab.

The equipment layout is similar in both nose units, each containing a Keith-Blackman traction motor blower, a Northey-Boyce exhauster, carbon dioxide fire-fighting bottles, and the inter-locomotive gangway connections. The cabs have the normal two seats, heaters, etc. The instrumentation and controls include a power controller and reversing switch in a pedestal unit, both being interlocked mechanically to prevent incorrect operation, the controller only capable of being moved when released by a key. Wheel-slip protection circuits automatically reduce tractive effort and illuminate a warning light. Additional lights give notice of engine shut-down, traction-motor blower failure, rise of engine water coolant temperature, and train-heating boiler shut down.

Operation of the controller-energised circuits through English Electric standard electro-pneumatic and electro-magnetic equipment controls engine speed between 450 and 850rpm, the loading being automatically adjusted so that

radiator compartment. Close fitting doors gave access to the cabs and engine compartment. Hatches in the bodyside are provided, as are roof hatches and removable roof sections to permit access and removal of equipment. Roof, cab doors, nose end-intercommunicating doors are of cast alloy. The underframe is welded-up from rolled steel sections as a single stressed unit. The engine fuel tank of 700gal capacity is located in the radiator compartment, while the space between the bogies carries an underslung 800gal water tank for providing train-heating boiler water, the tank being refillable by scoop from water troughs while troughs were still provided for steam locomotives or by normal methods

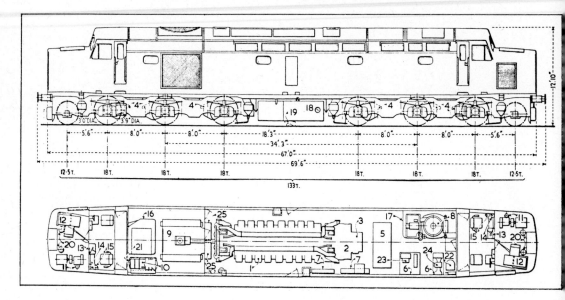

Fig 9: Diagram of the first successful Type 4 diesel on BR, the English Electric 2000bhp 1Co-Co1 diesel-electrics of class 40. Key: 1 Main engine; 2 Main generator; 3 Auxiliary generator; 4 Traction motor; 5 Equipment frame; 6 Batteries; 7 Resistances; 8 Train heating boiler; 9 Radiators; 10 Compressor; 11 Brake exhauster; 12 Traction-motor blower; 13 Controller; 14 Vacuum-brake valve; 15 Air-brake valve; 16 Engine fuel tank; 17 Boiler fuel tank; 18 Water tank; 19 Water pick-up; 20 Carbon dioxide cylinders; 21 Main reservoirs; 22 Toilet; 23 Load regulator; 24 Voltage regulator; 25 Header tank. *(Author's collection)*

the power delivered corresponds to selected engine speed.

The rear cab wall is a bulkhead giving access through a centre door to the engine room from the cab at one end and the radiator compartment from the other. The engine room houses the engine-generator set, main control cubicle, batteries, train-heating boiler and its fuel tank, toilet, and engine coolant and header tank.

The engine is the English Electric 16 SVT Mark II vee type unit rated at 2000bhp at 850rpm. This 16 cylinder unit is pressure charged by four Napier exhaust-gas turbo-chargers. The main generator is bolted to the engine; it is an English Electric type 822, self-ventilated, single-bearing, dc machine with a continuous rating of 1800amp at 730V, power output being varied by control of the diesel engine speed and generator field excitation. A dc auxiliary generator with self-ventilation is fitted. This has an output of 110V at a constant rate, being maintained by a carbon-pile voltage regulator. This supplies power for driving control gear, compressor, exhausters, blowers, and battery charging.

The radiator compartment contains Spiral Tube double-bank side-mounted radiators for cooling the engine lubricant and cooling water. Air is drawn across the radiators by a roof-mounted fan which expels it through the roof. The fan is driven through a right-angle gear box from the free-end of the engine. Coolant water temperature is controlled by a thermostatic by-pass valve. The radiator anti-frost shutters are controlled from the cab. Also contained in this compartment are the air compressor, engine fuel tanks, and main air reservoirs.

Traction motors are six EE type 526/5D axle-hung, nose-suspended machines mounted one to each driving axle. They are dc series-wound machines driving through single-reduction spur gears. They each have a continuous rating of 600amp at 300V. Field divert resistances were provided to allow simultaneous weakening of the traction motor field. Force-ventilation is taken from blowers in the nose compartments. The traction motors are connected in parallel across the main generator, in three series pairs.

The D200 bogies were found to be susceptible to stresses in their running gear and the suspension was modified. With a bogie having only primary suspension, body support prevented the bogies adjusting to bad track inequalities and vertical curves in hump yards, while the heavy

The first of the EE type 4s, No D200, on a demonstration run to Norwich, seen here just north of Colchester on 18 April 1958. *(British Railways)*

reverse-cambered laminated springs needed frequent attention. In a modification first introduced on locomotive D321 solid cross beams replaced the laminated springs, which in turn were replaced by helical springs. The placing of the beam over the axlebox close to the bogie frame plate, made the use of tandem helical springs necessary.

The combination of a hard-riding bogie and resulting vibrations caused another fault to develop with the six-pole traction motors, flash-overs at the higher end of the speed range. The D200s were designed to meet the BR require-ment of high tractive effort-high power, the main generator and traction motors being wound accordingly. A somewhat unstable weak field resulted and the six-pole motors, in a combination of bogie vibrations and dirty, worn commutators and brushes, were prone to flash over. As a result the LMR embarked on converting its fleet of D200s to four-pole motors purchased new from EE, the old motors being returned to EE for overhaul and re-use in the new D8000 locomotives then under delivery. The D200s concerned were identified at that time by a blue line painted under the locomotive number and by having their control cubicles painted

blue. These heavy plate-frame bogies were a mistake from the start when they were conceived by Bulleid for 10201-3, the D200s and the following 2300/2500bhp BR built units of classes 44-46 suffering accordingly. The bogies gave a good ride but punished locomotives and track, especially on tight curves, while the effort and time required to rerail one was usually accompanied by words which cannot be printed here!

Grease lubrication replaced oil on the pony truck swing-links and associated gear. The oil had been fed by a mechanical lubricator shaft-driven from a gear box with right-angle drive from the leading axle-box.

The D200s were modified as production progressed; one of the early alterations was the addition of anti-dilution trays to the high pressure fuel pipes, to prevent fuel reaching the engine sump, about three-quarters of the class being so fitted from new. Fuel injection systems for the earlier and later examples of the class varied in design.

From about the mid 1960s breakages of camshaft chains caused the fitting of fret-free chains and overcame the necessity to renew chains at 3600 engine hour examinations. Turbo-charger bearings and oil seals were renewed by a modified type early in the career of the class, while the common complaint of cold draughty cabs was cured by replacing engine-coolant and air-blower heating by electric heaters.

Another problem was the under-cooling of the

class, which were run with too high coolant water-temperatures, a fault not really taken seriously for rectification. Modifications to the coolant-water header tanks, resulting from a number of service failures due to loss of coolant because of imbalance between the twin water-pumps, necessitated the fitting of a new balancing pipe circuit between the tanks and the pumps. From September 1968 water pick-up gear was taken out and the air-supply pipes plugged. Troubles during 1974 with the cracking of cylinder-head covers saw the fitting of Mk III replacement covers, a practice being now extended to other members of the class.

Between 1955 and 1960 six orders were placed for locomotives of this type. The 200 locomotives which comprise the class have always remained on the same regional allocations: ER, NER, LMR, and ScR. Transfers between regions and depots occurred with the advent of later more powerful locomotives and electrification.

The ER received D200-9 from mid-March 1958, the batch going from Vulcan Foundry to Doncaster works for acceptance trials, a practice which continued for all the D200s. D200 went to Stratford shed on the GE section and, following crew training, took part in a demonstration run on 18 March between Liverpool Street and Norwich and back. The nine coach, 335 ton train was emblazoned 'First 2000hp Diesel London-Norwich, Progress by Great Eastern'. D200 demonstrated the inherent diesel accelerative powers by being able to pick up time on the banks and coast down the other side. Its start from Liverpool Street enabled Stratford 4 miles to be passed in 6½min, the 115 mile run taking 116min 21sec, including a 3½min stop at Ipswich. A maximum of 88½mph was attained.

D201 went to Hornsey GN line shed for crew training in late April, the remaining eight going to Stratford (D202-5) and Hornsey (D206-9). The GE units were put to work on the East Anglian, Norfolkman, Broadsman, and other important trains. On the GN, following test running on normal steam duties, plans to launch a new diesel-hauled Kings Cross-Sheffield Pullman service in the autumn to replace the GC route Master Cutler were made and trials conducted.

The first D200-hauled Flying Scotsman was on 21 June 1958 with D201 as far as Newcastle. The summer saw them on the White Rose between Kings Cross and Leeds, and even on High Dyke-Frodingham ore trains. The new

Master Cutler Pullman commenced with the 1958 winter timetable, being booked to stop at Retford and cover the 161½ mile Kings Cross-Sheffield route in 165min, 07.20 up and 19.20 down.

The five Hornsey D200s were given rosters of up to 4700 miles per week and included the Flying Scotsman, Tees Tyne Pullman, and other East Coast and Cambridge duties. Although these diagrams were not strictly adhered to because of availability problems and difficulty in filling five diagrams with five locomotives, their impact on the Kings Cross 8P and 7P Pacifics was startling for full diesel availability would leave 38 Pacifics with only 17 duties!

D237-59 was the next East Coast batch delivered between October 1959 and February 1960 to Gateshead and York sheds, apart from D255 allocated to the LMR fitted with electric train heating and an anti-slip device, and D248 with a different train heating boiler sent to Hornsey to join D201/6-9. By August 1959 the Talisman and Aberdonian too were being diesel hauled and, following crew training at Gateshead on empty stock, parcels and freights, D200s were put on normal Heaton and Gateshead Pacific turns, not taking up full London and Edinburgh diagrams until early 1960, followed by Newcastle-Birmingham and Liverpool trains.

York used its D200s on training to Scarborough before taking on some of its steam duties. In early 1960 D256-9 were loaned by York to the ScR at Haymarket for training in preparation for deliveries to Scotland. The ever widening activities of NER D200s took them to Lincoln and into Scotland by mid-1960.

The Gateshead diagrams gave the D200s up to 576 miles in 14 hours on Newcastle-Kings Cross round trips. By mid-1960 they were taking most of the weekday East Coast trains. The winter rosters gave them 4,716 miles per week. One duty, which included the up Flying Scotsman, provided a 786 mile turn in 24 hours. The Elizabethan Kings Cross-Edinburgh non-stop was still diagrammed for an A4 Pacific. Although the East Coast Pacifics had little diagrammed work of moment to do by 1961, diesel troubles saw them in large scale use on main line duties.

Early 1961 saw the introduction of both NER and LMR D200s on the accelerated Liverpool-Newcastle service. The cuts in timings varied from 13 to 83min. The LMR loaned D301/2 to Leeds Neville Hill shed in early 1961, and

No D286 takes a southbound train through Selby on
6 August 1960. Note the ladder on the nose front.
(Brian Webb)

A northbound coal train coasts through Morpeth curve
behind No 258 on 17 July 1970. *(Ian S. Carr)*

M Region named class 40 No 216 *Campania* runs into Newcastle Central via the High Level bridge with the 8.40 Liverpool-Newcastle on Sunday, 15 November 1970. *(Ian S. Carr)*

raining runs to Appleby and Lancaster were undertaken, while others for Holbeck men with York D200s took the class on to the Leeds-Carlisle line for the first time.

On the GE section good running with the class was common, and it was usual to employ them on the Norfolkman with up to 10 coaches, 360 tons gross, as opposed to nine with a Britannia Pacific. One of the interesting aspects of diesel working on the GE section was the somewhat limited distances involved. With the D200s working to Norwich, 115 miles, or 124 miles via Cambridge, it was still quite possible to give them diagrams of 3600-3900 miles each seven day period.

By 1962, with ten D200s on GE lines, they were handling Norwich, Kings Lynn, and Yarmouth trains from London, assisted by D6700s, and averaging 464 miles per day or in the case of a two-day London-Norwich diagram, 1034 miles in 48 hours.

An early 1961 run with D202 saw it pass Harold Wood, 14.95 miles from Liverpool Street, in 16min 48sec, at 73mph, while the 1 in 100 section of Brentwood Bank was surmounted at 53/55mph, Chelmsford being passed in 30min on a 35min schedule. Although not exceeding 73mph, the 68.80 miles to Ipswich were accomplished in 73½min against a timing of 81min. After Ipswich, 80-90mph running in the Diss area saw the train arrive at Norwich 10min early on a 127min schedule.

The D345-56 series for the NER in mid-1961 were the first to incorporate the centrally placed nose-mounted four-digit indicators, and they were built without the nose-end gangway door. They were allocated in part to Neville Hill, where they soon monopolised the Queen of Scots Pullman from June, and to York shed.

The running of D200s on the Darlington-York racetrack section was usually excellent. On Newcastle-Liverpool, trains were timed to cover the 44.10 miles with 10 to 11 coaches in 36min, and further on the route, over the Pennines

he inaugural reduced fare train, The Highwayman, departs from Sunderland on its Newcastle-London run behind class 40 No 346 on 4 May 1970. *(Ian S. Carr)*

between Huddersfield and Stalybridge, a notoriously damp route involving 1 in 96 and 1 in 105 grades to Marsden, 7.1 miles from Huddersfield, a 12min allowance was no mean feat, and this schedule was frequently undercut.

Deltic deliveries commenced in 1961, but the D200s handled about 60 per cent of East Coast duties that year. But 1962, with the Deltics taking a bigger hand and the introduction of BR built 2500bhp Peak class diesels, saw a decline of D200 use on principal trains, while the following year, with the 2750hp D1500s then appearing, and the final batch of East Coast D200s, D385-99, the class was down-graded so that their usefulness was spread to other depots. Thornaby shed on Tees-side used its examples on longer freight jobs and, once Healey Mills depot opened, a large allocation of D200s was moved there, again mostly for freight work.

An interesting underemployment of the NER D200s from York shed was on the two daily locomotive-hauled return trips between Malton and Whitby. These locomotives took over from B1 class 4-6-0s in the summer of 1964 continuing until the line's closure in 1965, running often with only three or four non-corridor coaches. The use of these units no doubt hastened the line's uneconomic ending.

In the late 1960s the ER's D200s were still to be found deputising for their 2500/2750bhp successors which were falling well below their anticipated reliability. On the GE section the batch of D200s was displaced by the D1500s which arrived in 1965. The position on the East Coast has remained the same since then, with the D200s very much in evidence on freight work and on summer passenger duties. By September 1975 the ER had 66 D200s on its books, based at such depots as Healey Mills, York, Gateshead.

The LMR took delivery between May and November 1959 of the batch D210-36, followed by D267-9/87-344 in 1960/1 (D305-24 coming from Robert Stephenson and Hawthorns, Darlington), and finally D369-84 in 1961/2. Of this total, plus D255, of 105 locomotives, D324-44 had the split-type, four digit, nose-mounted indicators mounted each side of the gangway doors, subsequent ones having the central four digit box and no doors. Talk of applying charge-air cooling to uprate their engines to 2400bhp in 1960 did not in practice materialise. Apart from D255, allocated to Derby for initial trials, all were for West Coast services from Euston, and were allocated initially to Camden, Willesden, Crewe, and

Carlisle Upperby. Later some found their way to Edge Hill and Longsight depots as deliveries proceeded.

These were the West Coast's first large diesels, and they were destined to monopolise the services for many years, plus inter-regional duties between Liverpool and Newcastle. They were soon on Anglo-Scottish trains as far as Carlisle, including the Royal Scot on occasions. Until August 1960 none had worked north of Carlisle, but on the 19th, D211 took the 16.15 Crewe-Glasgow, soon being followed by others on such duties as the Royal Scot loaded to 14 coaches of 510 tons gross. D200 units were able to run from Euston-Crewe with 9 coaches, 298 tons tare/310 tons gross, well inside the 188min allowance for the 158.1 miles. In 1960 they added Euston-Birmingham and Birmingham-Glasgow trains to their range, while the flood of them in service by this time saw them on up to 60 per cent of expresses and a number of fast freights.

Although the Royal Scot reverted to steam haulage in early 1961, D200s were often provided for the Caledonian and Mid-Day Scot. On the former, usually an 8 coach formation of 280 tons gross, the D200s were in their element when allowed 336min for the 299 miles Carlisle-Euston leg, 20min early arrivals at Euston being easily attained.

The Royal Highlander was a D200 duty for a period from Crewe to Inverness over a 391 mile route, involving four summits of 915, 1000, 1480 and 1315ft with grades of 1 in 75, 1 in 70, 1 in 60 northbound. After a nine-hour layover the locomotive worked south and was away from home for 30 hours 21min, or 672 miles of haulage.

By May 1961 the Euston-Blackpool and Blackpool-Manchester services were converted to D200 haulage, resulting in the class having about 80 per cent of West Coast express services. The only route on which they had not invaded in any number was the North Wales route to Holyhead, even though they were working the Irish Mail and Emerald Isle Express by mid-summer. In contrast during the early 1970s this route was to see one of their last regular passenger duties. During 1962 the arrival of 2300/2500bhp diesels on the West Coast was only a brief visitation, and they soon left for the Midland line, the West Coast preferring reliability to horsepower.

It was an English Electric locomotive which was involved in the great train robbery of 1963.

On 8 August, D326 was working the 18.50 Aberdeen/Glasgow-Euston West Coast Postal mail train when a most daring and well organised robbery was carried out. The thieves altered a signal to show red by using batteries, so stopping D326 and its train at Sears Crossing north of Cheddington in the early hours of the morning. The thieves overpowered the crew of D326, uncoupled the locomotive and the first two vehicles of the train, and forced them to drive forward to an isolated bridge where, after tying up the crew, they removed registered packets, banknotes, and jewellery valued at £2½ million, and made a getaway. D326 was later impounded by Scotland Yard and taken to Cheddington for examination.

The Stanier Coronation Pacifics were finally withdrawn in September 1964, leaving the field entirely to the D200s as the LMR's principal express locomotive, for although the threat of the D1500s was felt by 1965, they had only partial effect. In spite of the D200s being under-powered for the heavy loads they had to take over Shap and Beattock, it was not until the more powerful D400s arrived from English Electric that the reign of the D200s ended. Electrification south of Crewe moreover, completed in stages in 1964/6, had enabled them to be sent to new depots such as Bletchley, Springs Branch, and Carlisle, and their use on freight duties increasing accordingly. The general popularity and reliability is indicated by the fact that Crewe depot used locomotives D21? and D233 as the LMR Royal Train locomotive long after the arrival of their more modern 2700/2750bhp successors.

D322 was the only withdrawal by the autumn of 1975, following damage received at Warrington on, of all days, Friday, 13 May 1966! No D322 was heading the Euston-Stranraer boat train which was involved in collision near Acton Grange Junction, Moore when, due to a broken coupling, 23 wagons from a Northwich-St Helens soda-ash train broke away on the 1 in 135 gradient, running into the oncoming express, which was travelling slowly following a signal check. The first 20ft of D322 was completely crushed, and it was obviously beyond repair. It was taken to Crewe works and scrapped there, its official withdrawal date being 28 October 1967. By the end of 1967 the class had a total mileage of 114 million miles, more than any other diesel type on BR.

D400 class deliveries in 1968 saw the D200 off most regular West Coast jobs north of Crewe

LM Region class 40 D332, with divided indicator boxes, passes Dearness Valley with the 09.00 Liverpool-Newcastle diverted via Bishop Auckland on 10 September 1961. (Ian S. Carr)

a situation which was maintained through the first half of the current decade, but their use on freight work is still prolific and makes the class probably the most common Type 4 north of Crewe. It is indeed salutary to witness their use in emergencies replacing other diesel classes, or even on the front of electrically-hauled trains for diversions or when the overhead catenary has come down.

The Scottish Region allocation of Type 4 diesels has never been large, since most of the requirements for this class of power are in the areas south of Glasgow and Edinburgh where English-based units work through remanned by Scottish crews, sometimes as far north as Perth and Aberdeen.

All the Scottish Type 4 units, D200s and D1500s, are based either at Glasgow or Edinburgh depots, the former class always at Haymarket. This depot received D260-6 and D357-68 new in February-April 1960 and August-December 1961 respectively, and have retained them. After completion of the West Coast electrification to Scotland in May 1974,

several D200s and D1500s were moved to Scotland to offset the lack of through-working facilities from the West Coast route.

The Haymarket D200 Class units were always used on the East Coast route, both south and northwards, the latter increasing from 1961 when the Edinburgh and Glasgow-Aberdeen trains were gradually dieselised. In the summer they even penetrated to Scarborough on through workings, while their use on the Waverley route before its closure on Millerhill-Carlisle freights was common.

In 1963 D200s were sometimes seen on Glasgow/Buchanan Street-Aberdeen trains in the midst of A3 and A4 Pacifics; at the end of 1965 D200s and other units replaced the last Gresley Pacific outpost.

The D357-68 batch had centrally-mounted four-digit train indicator panels and, in 1965, the D260-6 batch was dealt with similarly, a process which necessitated the removal of the old gangway doors in the nose units.

None of the class have received electric train heating equipment nor slow speed control, but

Pushing a diesel brake tender before it, class 40 No
D347 heads an empty mineral train through Mirfield on
its way to Healey Mills yard on Thursday, 3 February
1966. *(Brian Webb)*

train air braking gear is being fitted.
Considerable variations in equipment and
locomotive weights exist within the class 40
units. Their duties on freight has seen removal
of train-heating boilers while the introduction of
air-braking on rolling stock has contributed to
the complication.

Units without boilers and retaining just
locomotive air brake and train vacuum brake
weigh 128 tons in working order and 124 tons
6 cwt empty; the same locomotive with straight
air/automatic air braking for itself, and
automatic air/air-continuous vacuum for the
train brakes, weighs 129 tons 12 cwt loaded and
125 tons 6 cwt empty, no boiler water or fuel
being carried in either case.

The class 40 had either the Vapor OK4625, or
the Clayton RO2500 Mk I train-heating boiler,
both necessitating the provision of 800 gallons of
boiler feed water and 200 gallons of boiler fuel
oil. This equipment raised the locomotive weight
to 133 tons loaded.

Addition of straight air/automatic air
locomotive braking, and automatic air/air-
continuous vacuum train braking pushed these
weights even higher to 134 tons in working
order.

Remarkably, 25 of the class received names
associated with the Shipping Industry and their
duties on the LMR on the Euston to Liverpool
services. D210-2 were named at special
ceremonies at Euston and Liverpool Riverside

stations in 1960, but the remainder had their
names fitted without ceremony at either Derby
or Crewe works between March 1961 and March
1963. Since 1970 various locomotives have been
at work without one or both nameplates, so the
position as to which ones still carry names in late
1975 is not clear.

There can be no reservation placed on the

**TABLE 8
MAIN DETAILS AND DIMENSIONS
OF D200 CLASS, NOW CLASS 40**

Description	Data
Axle layout	1Co-Co1
Engine model	16SVT Mk II
Engine rating	2000bhp at 850rpm
Length over buffers	69ft 6in
Overall width	9ft 0in
Overall height	12ft 10 3/8in
Wheel diameter (driving)	3ft 9in
Wheel diameter (guiding)	3ft 0in
Bogie pivots	34ft 3in
Bogie wheelbase (rigid)	16ft 0in
Bogie wheelbase (total)	21ft 0in
Total wheelbase	61ft 3in
Maximum speed	90 mph
Maximum tractive effort	52,000 lb at 21.1% adhesion
Continuous tractive effort	30,900 lb at 18mph
Continuous rail hp	1550
Locomotive fuel capacity	710 gals
Weight in working order depending on variations in installed equipment	124 tons 6 cwt to 134 tons 0 cwt
Train heating boiler (when fitted)	Vapor OK4625 or Clayton RO2500 Mk I
Boiler water capacity	800 gals
Boiler fuel capacity	200 gals

statement that the D200s or Class 40 was the best buy made by BR in its Type 4 range of diesel-electrics. They were the first really successful main line locomotives on BR, and in their earlier years had to put up with the death throes of a steam railway system and like their LMS and SR predecessors suffering indignities in sharing soot-laden maintenance facilities with steam; yet in spite of this, they attained high mileages.

Their now out-dated lumbering forms are still to be found hard at work in the Midlands, the North and in Scotland, mostly on freight work, and it is hoped that when their time comes for withdrawal, one will be preserved in our fine new National Railway Museum at York, so that future generations can see, and one hopes hear too, that familiar English Electric Vee engine whistle—from their turbo chargers—which heralds their approach on the line.

TABLE 9   D200 CLASS TYPE 4 – LATER BR CLASS 40

Original BR No	Works No VF or RSH	Works No Eng Elec	Date to Traffic	Reg New	Allocation Sep '75	Original BR No	Works No VF or RSH	Works No Eng Elec	Date to Traffic	Reg New	Allocation Sep '75
D200	VF D395	2367	3/58	E	LM	D251	VF D468	2773	12/59	NE	E
D201	VF D396	2368	4/58	E	LM	D252	VF D469	2774	12/59	NE	E
D202	VF D397	2369	4/58	E	E	D253	VF D470	2775	1/60	NE	E
D203	VF D398	2370	5/58	E	LM	D254	VF D471	2776	12/59	NE	E
D204	VF D399	2371	5/58	E	LM	D255	VF D472	2777	P1/60	LM	LM
D205	VF D400	2372	6/58	E	E	D256	VF D473	2778	1/60	NE	E
D206	VF D401	2373	7/58	E	E	D257	VF D474	2779	2/60	NE	E
D207	VF D402	2374	7/58	E	E	D258	VF D475	2780	2/60	NE	E
D208	VF D403	2375	8/58	E	LM	D259	VF D476	2781	2/60	NE	E
D209	VF D404	2376	9/58	E	LM	D260	VF D497	2782	P2/60	SC	SC
D210	VF D427	2666	P5/59	LM	LM	D261	VF D498	2783	P2/60	SC	SC
D211	VF D428	2667	P6/59	LM	LM	D262	VF D499	2784	P9/60	SC	SC
D212	VF D429	2668	P6/59	LM	LM	D263	VF D500	2785	P3/60	SC	SC
D213	VF D430	2669	P6/59	LM	LM	D264	VF D501	2786	P3/60	SC	SC
D214	VF D431	2670	P6/59	LM	LM	D265	VF D502	2787	P3/60	SC	SC
D215	VF D432	2671	P7/59	LM	LM	D266	VF D503	2788	P3/60	SC	SC
D216	VF D433	2672	P7/59	LM	LM	D267	VF D504	2789	P3/60	LM	E
D217	VF D434	2673	P7/59	LM	LM	D268	VF D505	2790	P4/60	LM	E
D218	VF D435	2674	P7/59	LM	LM	D269	VF D506	2791	P4/60	LM	E
D219	VF D436	2675	P7/59	LM	LM	D270	VF D507	2792	4/60	NE	E
D220	VF D437	2676	P8/59	LM	LM	D271	VF D508	2793	4/60	NE	E
D221	VF D438	2677	P8/59	LM	LM	D272	VF D509	2794	4/60	NE	SC
D222	VF D439	2678	P8/59	LM	LM	D273	VF D510	2795	5/60	NE	E
D223	VF D440	2679	P8/59	LM	LM	D274	VF D511	2796	5/60	NE	E
D224	VF D441	2680	P9/59	LM	LM	D275	VF D512	2797	5/60	NE	E
D225	VF D442	2681	P9/59	LM	LM	D276	VF D513	2798	5/60	NE	LM
D226	VF D443	2682	P9/59	LM	LM	D277	VF D514	2799	5/60	NE	E
D227	VF D444	2683	P9/59	LM	LM	D278	VF D515	2800	6/60	NE	E
D228	VF D445	2684	P9/59	LM	LM	D279	VF D516	2801	6/60	NE	LM
D229	VF D446	2685	P9/59	LM	LM	D280	VF D517	2802	6/60	NE	E
D230	VF D447	2686	P10/59	LM	LM	D281	VF D518	2803	6/60	NE	E
D231	VF D448	2687	P10/59	LM	LM	D282	VF D519	2804	6/60	NE	LM
D232	VF D449	2688	P10/59	LM	LM	D283	VF D520	2805	7/60	NE	E
D233	VF D450	2689	P10/59	LM	LM	D284	VF D521	2806	7/60	NE	E
D234	VF D451	2690	P10/59	LM	LM	D285	VF D522	2807	7/60	NE	E
D235	VF D452	2691	P10/59	LM	LM	D286	VF D523	2808	7/60	NE	E
D236	VF D453	2692	P11/59	LM	E	D287	VF D524	2809	P8/60	LM	LM
D237	VF D454	2693	10/59	NE	E	D288	VF D526	2811	P8/60	LM	LM
D238	VF D455	2694	10/59	NE	E	D289	VF D525	2810	P9/60	LM	SC
D239	VF D456	2695	10/59	NE	E	D290	VF D527	2812	P9/60	LM	LM
D240	VF D457	2715	10/59	NE	E	D291	VF D528	2813	P9/60	LM	LM
D241	VF D458	2716	10/59	NE	SC	D292	VF D529	2814	P9/60	LM	E
D242	VF D459	2717	11/59	NE	LM	D293	VF D530	2815	P10/60	LM	LM
D243	VF D460	2718	11/59	NE	LM	D294	VF D531	2816	P10/60	LM	LM
D244	VF D461	2719	11/59	NE	LM	D295	VF D532	2817	P10/60	LM	LM
D245	VF D462	2720	11/59	NE	LM	D296	VF D533	2818	P10/60	LM	LM
D246	VF D463	2721	11/59	NE	E	D297	VF D534	2819	P11/60	LM	LM
D247	VF D464	2722	11/59	NE	E	D298	VF D535	2820	P11/60	LM	LM
D248	VF D465	2723	11/59	NE	E	D299	VF D536	2821	P11/60	LM	LM
D249	VF D466	2724	11/59	NE	E	D300	VF D537	2822	P11/60	LM	E
D250	VF D467	2772	12/59	NE	E	D301	VF D538	2823	P11/60	LM	SC

Table 9 Cont. D200 Class Type 4 — Later BR Class 40

Original BR No	Works No VF or RSH	Works No Eng Elec	Date to Traffic	Reg New	Allocation Sep '75	Original BR No	Works No VF or RSH	Works No Eng Elec	Date to Traffic	Reg New	Allocation Sep '75
D302	VF D539	2824	P12/60	LM	E	D371	VF D667	3117	P13/61	LM	LM
D303	VF D540	2825	P12/60	LM	SC	D372	VF D668	3118	P1/62	LM	LM
D304	VF D541	2826	P12/60	LM	LM	D373	VF D669	3119	P1/62	LM	SC
D305	RSH 8135	2725	P10/60	LM	LM	D374	VF D670	3120	P1/62	LM	LM
D306	RSH 8136	2726	P11/60	LM	LM	D375	VF D671	3121	P2/62	LM	LM
D307	RSH 8137	2727	P11/60	LM	LM	D376	VF D672	3122	P2/62	LM	E
D308	RSH 8138	2728	P12/60	LM	LM	D377	VF D673	3123	P2/62	LM	LM
D309	RSH 8139	2729	P12/60	LM	LM	D378	VF D674	3124	P2/62	LM	LM
D310	RSH 8140	2730	P12/60	LM	LM	D379	VF D675	3125	P2/62	LM	LM
D311	RSH 8141	2731	P13/60	LM	LM	D380	VF D676	3126	P3/62	LM	LM
D312	RSH 8142	2732	P13/60	LM	LM	D381	VF D677	3127	P3/62	LM	LM
D313	RSH 8143	2733	P13/60	LM	LM	D382	VF D678	3128	P3/62	LM	LM
D314	RSH 8144	2734	P13/60	LM	LM	D383	VF D679	3129	P3/62	LM	E
D315	RSH 8145	2850	P1/61	LM	LM	D384	VF D680	3130	P4/62	LM	SC
D316	RSH 8146	2851	P1/61	LM	LM	D385	VF D681	3131	3/62	NE	LM
D317	RSH 8147	2852	P2/61	LM	LM	D386	VF D682	3132	4/62	NE	LM
D318	RSH 8148	2853	P2/61	LM	LM	D387	VF D683	3133	4/62	NE	E
D319	RSH 8149	2854	P3/61	LM	LM	D388	VF D684	3134	4/62	NE	LM
D320	RSH 8150	2855	P3/61	LM	LM	D389	VF D685	3135	5/62	NE	LM
D321	RSH 8151	2856	P4/61	LM	LM	D390	VF D686	3136	5/62	NE	LM
D322	RSH 8152	2857	P4/61	LM	With-drawn	D391	VF D687	3137	5/62	NE	LM
						D392	VF D688	3138	5/62	NE	E
D323	RSH 8153	2858	P5/61	LM	LM	D393	VF D689	3139	6/62	NE	E
D324	RSH 8154	2859	P7/61	LM	E	D394	VF D690	3140	6/62	NE	E
D325	VF D621	3071	P13/60	LM	LM	D395	VF D691	3141	6/62	NE	E
D326	VF D622	3072	P13/60	LM	LM	D396	VF D692	3142	7/62	NE	E
D327	VF D623	3073	P13/60	LM	LM	D397	VF D693	3143	7/62	NE	E
D328	VF D624	3074	P1/61	LM	LM	D398	VF D694	3144	8/62	NE	E
D329	VF D625	3075	P1/61	LM	LM	D399	VF D695	3145	9/62	NE	E
D330	VF D626	3076	P2/61	LM	LM						
D331	VF D627	3077	P2/61	LM	LM						
D332	VF D628	3078	P2/61	LM	LM						
D333	VF D629	3079	P2/61	LM	LM						
D334	VF D630	3080	P3/61	LM	LM						
D335	VF D631	3081	P3/61	LM	LM						
D336	VF D632	3082	P3/61	LM	LM						
D337	VF D633	3083	P3/61	LM	LM						
D338	VF D634	3084	P4/61	LM	LM						
D339	VF D635	3085	P4/61	LM	LM						
D340	VF D636	3086	P4/61	LM	LM						
D341	VF D637	3087	P5/61	LM	LM						
D342	VF D638	3088	P5/61	LM	SC						
D343	VF D639	3089	P5/61	LM	LM						
D344	VF D640	3090	P5/61	LM	LM						
D345	VF D641	3091	5/61	NE	E						
D346	VF D642	3092	5/61	NE	E						
D347	VF D643	3093	5/61	NE	E						
D348	VF D644	3094	6/61	NE	E						
D349	VF D645	3095	6/61	NE	E						
D350	VF D646	3096	6/61	NE	E						
D351	VF D647	3097	6/61	NE	E						
D352	VF D648	3098	7/61	NE	E						
D353	VF D649	3099	7/61	NE	E						
D354	VF D650	3100	7/61	NE	E						
D355	VF D651	3101	8/61	NE	E						
D356	VF D652	3102	8/61	NE	E						
D357	VF D653	3103	P9/61	SC	SC						
D358	VF D654	3104	P9/61	SC	SC						
D359	VF D655	3105	P10/61	SC	SC						
D360	VF D656	3106	P10/61	SC	SC						
D361	VF D657	3107	P10/61	SC	SC						
D362	VF D658	3108	P11/61	SC	SC						
D363	VF D659	3109	P11/61	SC	SC						
D364	VF D660	3110	P11/61	SC	SC						
D365	VF D661	3111	P11/61	SC	SC						
D366	VF D662	3112	P12/61	SC	SC						
D367	VF D663	3113	P12/61	SC	SC						
D368	VF D664	3114	P12/61	SC	SC						
D369	VF D665	3115	P13/61	LM	E						
D370	VF D666	3116	P13/61	LM	LM						

TABLE 10
LIST OF NAMES CARRIED BY
D200 CLASS LOCOMOTIVES

Locomotive Number	Date Named	Name
D210	12/5/60	Empress of Britain
D211	20/9/60	Mauretania
D212	20/9/60	Aureol
D213	6/62	Andania
D214	5/61	Antonia
D215	5/62	Aquitania
D216	5/62	Campania
D217	5/62	Carinthia
D218	7/61	Carmania
D219	6/62	Caronia
D220	2/63	Franconia
D221	3/61	Ivernia
D222	10/62	Laconia
D223	5/61	Lancastria
D224	8/62	Lucania
D225	3/62	Lusitania
D227	6/62	Parthia
D228	9/62	Samaria
D229	3/63	Saxonia
D230	4/61	Scythia
D231	5/62	Sylvania
D232	3/61	Empress of Canada
D233	9/61	Empress of England
D234	5/62	Accra
D235	5/62	Apapa

Notes: D210: Named at Euston Station by Mr N. Crump of Canadian Pacific Steamship Co.

D211: Named at Liverpool Riverside Station by Sir J. L. Brocklebank, Chairman of Cunard Steamship Co.

D212: Named at Liverpool Riverside Station by M. Glaister, Director of Elder Dempster Line.

CHAPTER 8

THE 'SMALL DELTIC' LOCOMOTIVES

Some of the last locomotives to be delivered of the 1955 pilot scheme were the ten 'small Deltic' locomotives numbered D5900-9. Intended for use on the ER, the locomotives were generally fairly conventional mechanically, apart from the unconventional engine.

The locomotive body was full width, and comprised a central machinery compartment flanked by end cabs and a short nose compartment with gangway connections. The underframe was of welded construction made up of two inner I-section beams and two outer channel-sections, with welded cross-members and drag-boxes. The body side frames were pre-fabricated and welded to the underframe. The roof over the equipment section was removable in sections to facilitate insertion and removal of engine, generator, and train-heating boiler.

Cab access was by side doors, and an extra side door provided access to the engine room. Fuel tanks and water tanks were hung from the underframe, being recessed at one side to carry the battery boxes. Total fuel capacity for both engine and the train-heating boiler was 550gal.

The bogies employed welded and riveted side-frames of box section with welded cross members riveted to the sides. The bolster was carried on semi-elliptical springs supported by planks and inclined swing links; lateral movement of the bolster was limited by rubber blocks. Springing between frame and wheels was in the form of nests of helical springs located between the frame and an equalising beam on each side, the beams being underslung from the SKF roller-bearing axle-boxes. Air braking was fitted for the locomotive and vacuum for the train.

Power was provided by a nine-cylinder Napier Deltic 18 piston two-stroke opposed-piston engine of model T9-29. This was a three-line inverted triangular engine set to give 1100bhp at 1600rpm. Phasing gears at the driving end of the engine linked the three crankshafts to combine their outputs in a common driving gear through which the engine power was transmitted to the main generator. Turbo-blowers of Napier make were fitted on the engine free end, port timing, by the pistons, being arranged to give a complete scavenge as well as pressure-charging.

Engine oil and water cooling was carried out in a roof-mounted double-bank radiator with thermostatic water temperature control. Manually operated shutters were fitted over the radiators. External air to the inside passed through panel filters of oil-wetted type fitted on the engine intake side panels.

The main generator, bolted to a housing on the engine, together with a top-mounted auxiliary generator, formed one unit with the engine; the generator had separate excitation, the output being varied by control of engine speed and main generator field excitation.

The auxiliary generator was driven by an auxiliary shaft from the engine phasing gearbox, putting out a constant 110V by a carbon-pile regulator, supplying current for battery charging, control system, driving vacuum-brake exhausters, train heating boiler controls, lighting and heating.

Four force-ventilated, axle-hung, nose-suspended traction motors with single reduction gear drive were connected across the main generator in two parallel groups of two motors in series; field weakening was brought in at the upper part of the locomotive speed range. Wheel slip protection circuits were included, and visual indication was given by warning lights. All the control gear except the two master controllers in the driving cab was contained in one cubicle in the engine room which formed part of one driving cab rear bulkhead.

There were the usual electro-pneumatic and electro-magnetic contactors and relays. Stepless variation of engine speed over the 600-1600rpm range was provided, the loading being adjusted automatically to cause the engine to deliver the maximum power corresponding to the selected rpm. The control system included a pedal-controlled deadman's system.

Some auxiliaries were driven by the engine through a power take-off from the free end of the engine, which led to an auxiliary drive gearbox. Horizontal drives were taken to the Westinghouse air compressor via a plate clutch and to one traction motor blower; a vertical shaft with flexible drive coupling went to the roof-mounted radiator fan. The second traction-motor blower was driven from an extension of

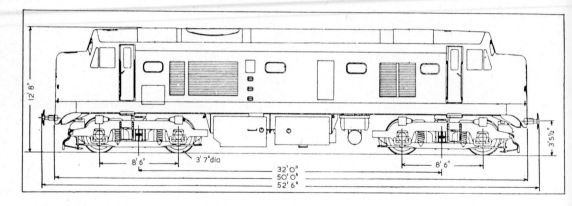

Fig 10: General layout diagram of the 1000bhp Type 2 'Baby Deltic', Bo-Bo of 1959, later class 23. Key: 1 Engine; 2 Main generator; 3 Auxiliary generator; 4 Traction motors (4); 5 Control cubicle; 6 Batteries; 7 Resistances; 8 Radiator panels; 9 Radiator fan; 10 Water pressure filling; 11 Auxiliary drive gear box; 12 Air compressor; 13 Vacuum exhausters (2); 14 Traction motor blowers; 15 Fuel tank; 16 Air filters; 17 Master controller; 18 Air brake valve; 19 Vacuum brake valve; 20 Fuel pressure filling; 21 Instrument panel; 22 Handbrake; 23 Fire extinguishers; 24 CO_2 equipment; 25 Train heating boiler; 26 Water tank; 27 Driver's seat; 28 Assistant's seat; 29 Lub. oil tank; 30 Reservoirs; 31 Breakfast cooker. *(Author's collection)*

the auxiliary generator armature shaft. The Reavell exhausters had their own electric motors. A Stone-Vapor train-heating boiler of 1,750 lb per hour capacity was fitted.

The D5900s, or 'Baby Deltics' as they were usually called, proved to have a weight exceeding that stipulated by BR and a 1958 delivery date was abandoned after D5900 had been rejected by BR because of excess weight largely it seems by over-enthusiasm at English Electric, in which the design team were misled by the lightweight Deltic engine. The result was that the locomotives were held at Vulcan Foundry to allow investigations into ways of lightening them to be carried out.

Work undertaken to reduce the weight included cutting holes in some items of the superstructure, bogies, etc, and fitting of lightweight Oleo-Pneumatic buffers. This was to prove of no avail as the Eastern Region, recipients of the class, still found them too heavy for cross-river, London area inter-regional freight duties to the SR where more limited axle-loadings applied on certain routes. A good-looking locomotive was produced nevertheless, with rather stubby nose units, finished in BR dark green with a broad off-white band at the base of the body-sides, together with an integrated frontal red band at the buffers.

They were delivered to Hornsey shed during April-June 1959, to be used on passenger work, particularly outer suburban trains and Cambridge duties from Kings Cross. Their work

was poor for the first four years, due mainly to trouble with cylinder liners and pistons, and to engine seizure through coolant loss arising from the fracture of the accessory drive shaft from the engine, damaging the coolant inlet pipe; the result was numerous visits to Stratford works for engine changing. In 1960 alone there were about 30 visits to works, some locomotives four or five times. This continued through 1961/2, an almost impossible situation for regular rostering. Their unreliability saw them employed in practice mostly on local freight and Kings Cross empty carriage workings, where irregularity was not quite so noticeable. On occasions they worked on the Hertford branch passenger trains and also on some Broad Street suburban duties.

Matters came to a head in 1962 when a spate of failures on Royston and Hitchin trains caused Hornsey to relegate the class as a whole to local goods and shunting work, their duties being taken over by the only available locomotives, a batch of English Electric Type 1 units, without train-heating equipment. The comments of passengers travelling in these Type 1 hauled trains on cool spring mornings were rather caustic!

'Baby Deltic' No D5908 on a Baldock-Kings Cross local train passes Oakleigh Park in September 1960. *(Derek Cross)*.

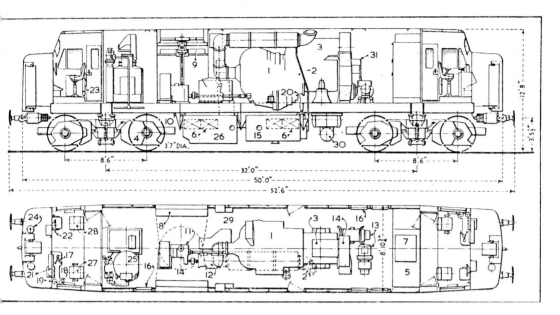

By early 1963, six of the small Deltics were stored at Stratford, their fate being sealed during July 1963 when D5905, the last to remain at work, ceased operating too. The whole class went back to Vulcan Foundry for modifications during July/August.

The engine refurbishing programme took about 12 months; while at VF they lost their nose-end gangway doors and had four-digit indicators fitted. No D5905/9 returned to Doncaster works for acceptance trials in June/July 1964, but the last, No 5901, was not returned to service until May 1965, by which time all were based at the new Finsbury Park diesel depot. They now sported a livery similar to the large Deltics, but although they now operated more successfully, at no time did they emulate their larger brethren.

Between 1963 and 1968 they were much in evidence at Kings Cross on station pilot, suburban trains, on trains to Cambridge and, on occasions, to Peterborough. They also worked to Broad Street on suburban trains and some were allocated to Hitchin for this purpose.

A refurbished class 23, No D5903 in Doncaster works in January 1966. Note removal of nose gangway doors and provision of indicator box. *(Norman Skinner)*

The Class 23s, as they had become, being a small non-standard type, were doomed under the BR diesel locomotive rationalisation plan, D5906 being withdrawn during September 1968. Mid-1969 found four still at work, and during August some found their way over the Metropolitan widened lines to Moorgate, their first visit for many years. D5901 was transferred in August 1969 to the BR Research Centre at Derby, leaving D5902/5/9 still in traffic. D5909 had been repainted following overhaul at Doncaster works during 1968, and was the only member of the class to run in BR rail-blue livery, although some others did sport the new symbol with their two-tone green livery. It was the last to remain in traffic, running until March 1971. The last two, D5905/9, were to remain dumped at Stratford until early 1973 when they were sold for scrap.

D5901, or 5901 as it is at the time of writing in autumn 1975, is still with the BR Centre at Derby, its chief task being haulage of the Mobile Adhesion Testing Laboratory Train, incorporating a Tribometer vehicle to survey wheel-rail adhesion on a 12-monthly basis over a route carrying all types of traffic.

The class was not the best of the English Electric breed and was in fact very untypical. The application of such an engine to a low-power locomotive was probably not a good choice, and it seemed an inordinately complex and costly solution to a basic requirement.

TABLE 11
MAIN DETAILS AND DIMENSIONS OF D5900 CLASS, LATER CLASS 23

Description	Data
Axle layout	Bo-Bo
Engine model	T9-29
Engine rating	1100BHP at 1600rpm
Locomotive weight, in working order	73tons 17cwt
Brakes, locomotive	Air
Brakes, train	Vacuum
Train heating	Stone-Vapor boiler
Boiler water tank capacity	500gals
Length over buffers	52ft 6in
Overall width	8ft 10¾in
Overall height	12ft 8in
Wheel diameter	3ft 7in
Bogie pivots	32ft 0in
Bogie wheelbase	8ft 6in
Total wheelbase	40ft 6in
Maximum speed	75mph
Maximum tractive effort	47,000 lb
Continuous tractive effort	30,600 lb at 10mph
Locomotive and boiler fuel capacity	550gals

TABLE 12
D5900 CLASS TYPE 2, LATER BR CLASS 23

Original BR No	Works No Vul Fdry	Works No Eng Elec	Date to Traffic	Regional Allocation	Date Wdn
D5900	D417	2377	5/59	E	12/68
D5901	D418	2378	5/59	E	12/69
D5902	D419	2379	5/59	E	11/69
D5903	D420	2380	4/59	E	12/68
D5904	D421	2381	4/59	E	1/69
D5905	D422	2382	5/59	E	2/71
D5906	D423	2383	5/59	E	9/68
D5907	D424	2384	5/59	E	10/68
D5908	D425	2385	5/59	E	3/69
D5909	D426	2386	6/59	E	3/71

*D5901 is still in Departmental stock as at 1975 and based at the BR Research Centre, Derby.

CHAPTER 9

THE UBIQUITOUS CLASS 37 LOCOMOTIVES

No provision was made in the 1955 pilot scheme diesel locomotive orders in the power capacity of 1500-1800bhp, a range with a good potential for a general purpose locomotive. The first order for the English Electric design in this range was placed in early 1959 for 42 locomotives Nos D6700-41, and grouped within the Type 3 classification. Initial deliveries—D6700 was the first in December 1960—were from the Vulcan Foundry, later joined by Stephenson and Hawthorns.

They are suitable for coupling with all other English Electric classes, and in general appearance are similar but shorter than the D200 class. The mechanical design is based upon a fabricated underframe of three sections, consisting of two longitudinal joists in the centre supporting the power unit, fuel and water tanks, and two identical outer sections over the bogies. Cross connection is by transoms of welded construction to form the bogie pivot centres; an adequate number of cross-stretchers also is provided. The drag-boxes are welded at both ends of the frame and carry standard BR buffing and draw gear; provision for future centre couplers is made.

The fuel and water tanks are underslung in the centre of the underframe. The superstructure had pre-fabricated side framing attached to the underframe by welding. Removable roof sections are provided for maintenance purposes. A driving cab and nose unit is provided at both ends. Cab access is by side doors. Access to the equipment compartments is from the cab via the rear cab-bulkhead door.

No 1 nose accommodates a gangway connection on locomotives D6700-6818, and an air-compressor, and traction motor blower for the adjacent bogie. The first 119 locomotives have split-type four-digit indicators, two digits on each side of the nose gangway doors; the remaining locomotives, without gangway doors, have the centrally placed four-digit indicator and warning horns on the cab roof. Behind the bulkhead of No 1 cab is the cooling group, comprising bodyside radiators and roof mounted fan. In the engine room, together with the engine/generator set and train-heating-boiler (where fitted), the main control cubicle

forms the rear bulkhead for No 2 cab. The second nose unit houses gangway connection (if fitted), vacuum exhausters, and the second traction motor blower group. Driving controls are built into a desk similar to those of the D200 class.

Each of the bogies has three motored axles, and are of equalised type with swingbolsters, being developed from those of the prototype Deltic locomotive. The body is carried on four side bearers on each bogie bolster, and the load is transmitted through four nests of coil springs to two spring planks suspended by swing links from the bogie frame. Dampers are fitted between the bolster and the spring plank adjacent to each of the four nests of coil springs. From the bogie solebars loading is distributed through four pairs of coil springs to forged steel equalising beams underslung from the roller bearing axleboxes. The bogie frames are of fabricated construction with box-section sole-bars to which the transoms and headstocks are riveted.

Box section fabrications are also used for the bolsters, traction motor cooling air being ducted through the hollow members to serve two motors on each bogie, final connection being by flexible bellows. Air for the third motor is via special ducting and bellows. Later locomotives have cast steel bogie frames.

Brake equipment is by Westinghouse, with air brakes on the locomotive, vacuum for the train, being supplied by a Worthington-Simpson compressor in the case of the former, this also including air for the horns, sanding, and control gear. The latter was provided by two Northey flange-mounted exhausters motored from the 110V dc auxiliary supply. A deadman's pedal is provided at each driving position.

The engine is the English Electric 12 CSVT unit with 12 cylinders in 60 degree vee form giving 1750bhp at 850rpm. Two Napier turbo-blowers of exhaust-gas type are fitted, the air being charge-air cooled after leaving the turbo-blowers and before entering the engine cylinders.

The main generator is bolted solidly to the engine and, together with an auxiliary generator overhung on the main generator, forms a

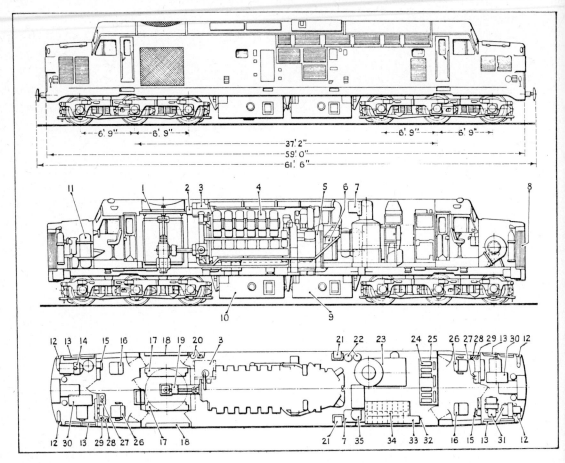

Fig. 11: General arrangement of D6700 or class 37 1750bhp Co-Co diesel-electric built to a total of 309 examples between 1960 and 1965, and rated as one of the most successful of BR diesel locomotives. Key: 1 Radiator fan; 2 Radiator header tank; 3 Emergency fuel tank; 4 Engine (12CSVT); 5 Main generator (EE822/109); 6 Auxiliary generator (EF911/5C); 7 Lavatory header tank; 8 Flexible gangway; 9 Water tank (800 gallons); 10 Fuel tank (920 gallons); 11 Main reservoirs; 12 Sandbox fillers; 13 Air filters; 14 Compressor; 15 Hand brake; 16 Assistant's seat; 17 Radiators; 18 Radiator shutters; 19 Radiator fan drive; 20 Engine fuel supply unit; 21 Water filling chute; 22 Supply reservoirs; 23 Train-heating boiler; 24 Field resistors; 25 Main equipment frame; 26 Driver's seat; 27 Master controller; 28 Air brake valve; 29 Vacuum brake valve; 30 Traction motor blowers; 31 Exhausters; 32 Westinghouse equipment; 33 Auxiliary equipment frame; 34 Batteries; 35 Toilet. *(Author's collection)*

compact integral power unit. The engine-generator set is supported on resilient bearers to account for flexing of the underframe.

Cooling radiators are mounted in pairs, one behind the other on both body sides. The outer panels are interconnected and cool the circulating water for the charge-air coolers and engine oil cooler. The two inner panels, also interconnected, are for engine jacket and turbo-blower water cooling. Air is drawn across the radiators by a mechanically driven roof mounted fan, being expelled through a roof mounted grille. Each pair of radiator panels has anti-frost shutters operated from the cab. Oil wetted filters in the bodysides filter all air taken into the locomotive interior.

The main generator is of type EE 822/109, being a dc self-ventilated, single-bearing machine continuously rated at 1107kW at 850rpm. In addition to a separately excited field winding which is used for normal running, it is provided with a series field winding used with the battery for engine starting. The auxiliary generator is a dc self-ventilated unit with a constant voltage of 110V, being maintained by a carbon-pile voltage regulator.

Six nose-suspended 600A traction motors drive via single-reduction gearing, being interchangeable with those fitted to the Deltic locomotives and of type EE 598/A.

Control gear is mainly housed in a single cubicle which faces into No 2 cab and placed across the locomotive. The remainder, together with the load regulator, is placed in a case mounted on the locomotive side above the battery box on the opposite side to the train-heating boiler.

The driver's controls are similar to those of the D200 class, but the associated load-regulator is activated by hydraulically-driven vane motor, operated by the governor from the engine oil pressure, the first time that this form of control was fitted on a BR English Electric locomotive.

The first of the D6700 (or Class 37 as they are known) units was delivered to Doncaster works on 2 December 1960 for its acceptance trials. The testing undertaken included static tests of all equipment and running tests, usually to Newark, with empty stock trains. D6701/2 followed soon after, and all three were allocated to Stratford shed of the ER, taking up work there during January 1961. Initial crew training completed, the locomotives were soon running such trains as the 13.30 Liverpool Street-Norwich and 17.56 Liverpool Street-Cambridge as training turns.

The ER was allocated the first 30, D6700-29 being based also at March, Ipswich, and Norwich sheds. Deliveries were confused and delayed during March and April, because of the discovery of fractures in the bogie frames and the return of those already delivered to Vulcan Foundry for attention. Apart from this and minor teething problems, the D6700s were an immediate success on all forms of duties, and soon averaged 342 miles per day.

The D6730-41 batch were for the NER at Hull Dairycoates shed, the first arriving in October 1961, and driver training starting immediately on the coast line through Bridlington to Scarborough.

As the allocation increased, the class was to be seen on freights to Doncaster and the West Riding, and also on the Hull-Doncaster run of Hull-Kings Cross trains such as the Yorkshire Pullman. During May 1962, D6735/6 were lent to Thornaby shed on Tees-side, pending an allocation there to permit crew training. Mid-1962 saw the GE area units in intensive use, mostly on freight work, but on Saturdays they often monopolised the Clacton interval service trains between Liverpool Street and Clacton.

During July 1962 the steady flow of D6700s from Vulcan Foundry was joined by those from the Darlington plant of Robert Stephenson & Hawthorns Ltd, the first of these going to the NER at Thornaby as expected. This batch,

Down view of fabricated and part riveted three axle bogie as fitted to BR classes 37 and 55, and also to the prototype locomotive DP2, all of which were Co-Co units. Note arrangement of traction motors and fabricated bogie bolster used as air duct for traction motor cooling. *(GEC Traction Ltd)*

D6769-95, was also allocated to Gateshead and Hull. D6742-54 were sent from VF to Sheffield Tinsley, and D6755-68 to Thornaby to join the RSH units. By this time the sphere of operation was widening, especially with excursion traffic during the summer months.

During September 1962 the Western Region's large scale diesel-hydraulic programme was proving costly to carry through and it looked even then, as far as BR was concerned, that the days of the diesel-hydraulic were numbered. Accordingly D6742/3 from Tinsley were sent to Cardiff Canton shed, South Wales, for trials during September/October 1962, returning in April 1963.

The Eastern and North Eastern Regions took

In spite of its fleet of diesel-hydraulics, the WR undertook high-speed tests with paired English Electric class 37 locomotives Nos D6881/2 during June 1965. Here they are seen near West Ealing on one 100mph run with a train including the XP64 prototype coaches. *(British Railways)*

119 (D6700-6818) D6700s by March 1963 and were getting excellent results, Tinsley using some of its locomotives on the Master Cutler to Kings Cross, while GE section locomotives were working as far as Sheffield with the Harwich-Liverpool boat trains.

With the immediate needs of the above regions satisfied, the beginning of the end for the WR diesel-hydraulics was signalled. Both English Electric works concentrated their rapid deliveries of D6700s and undivided attention on the WR, initially with an order for 100 locomotives numbered D6819-D6918.

The first deliveries were in March to Cardiff Canton, soon followed by allocations to Landore shed, Swansea. As numbers increased, D6742/3 were returned to the ER, in April 1963. The WR D6700s were employed mostly on freight work and on the South Wales Valleys coal trains, many soon being based at such sub-sheds as Radyr.

With deliveries from two EE workshops simultaneously rapid progress in dieselisation was achieved, use of Class 37s was soon extended to steelworks traffic, notably from Newport docks with iron ore for Spencer steelworks at Llanwern, and coal from the Eastern Valleys collieries to the same works, and to Margam. Some worked in multiple pairs. The Newport-Llanwern iron ore traffic operated on a push-pull system with locomotive and brakevan at each end of trains with a gross loading including locomotives, wagons and ore, of 1,700 tons. Up to 16 trains a day with a 1 hour 50 min round trip timing were operated.

West Wales was soon penetrated by Landore locomotives working to Neyland, Tenby, Milford Haven, and Carmarthen. In 1963 the Eastern and NE units were working further afield with Thornaby locomotives going to Skipton on Tees Yard-Barrow in Furness freights, and Stratford examples with West Midlands oil and gas trains heading down the LM main line as far as Rugby.

Early 1964 saw South Wales deliveries

running at two to three a week, all going to Canton or Landore, but out-stationed at many sub-sheds. Those at Newport Ebbw Jcn were taking ore to Ebbw Vale, one locomotive at each end, as in steam practice. About 100 D6700s were at work on the WR by mid-1964; another depot, Bristol Bath Road, took one for the first time in May but it was outstationed at Bromsgrove as a banking locomotive for the Lickey Incline, crew training being in progress in June/July. By late August four were expected to take over from the 9400 Class 0-6-0PTs and the Class 9F 2-10-0 which had acted as bankers for some years.

Final deliveries took place in November 1965 when D6608 arrived at Doncaster for its acceptance trials. By 1964 when 230 locomotives had been delivered, they were averaging 100,000 miles per year, with a fleet mileage of over 13 million miles.

As part of the WR speed-up of its passenger services, mid-1965 saw high speed trials with D6700s in multiple between Bristol and Paddington, and the West of England and Paddington. On 3 June D6881/2 in a 3500bhp combination took an eight-coach train, the XP64 prototype set and a dynamometer car, weighing 350 tons, from Paddington to Plymouth and back. In the down direction the train ran via Westbury, and covered the 173.5 miles to Exeter in 132min 18sec, giving an average of 78.6mph with a top speed of 92mph. The 226 miles to Plymouth were covered at an average of 69mph.

On the up run, from Taunton the route was via Bristol and Bath, with a call only at Bristol between Plymouth and London. This gave two non-stop sections of 127.6 and 118.3 miles, the latter covered in 86min 36sec being the fastest timing between Bristol and Paddington at an

Class 37s fore and aft with a load of hoppers for BSC Spencer Steelworks at Llanwern near Newport on the Western Region. These trains operate quick turnround shuttle services between Newport Docks and Llanwern involving reversals. *(GEC Traction Ltd)*

average of 82.6mph. With the special easing of the 90mph line speed limit for about 60 route miles, maximum speeds of 102 and 104mph respectively were reached in two places on the Challow-Goring section. This illustrated just what a maid-of-all-work diesel-electric locomotive can do, and gives strength to a BR district motive power man who said 'give me a fleet of 6700s for all my shed workings'.

When D6988 was delivered to the WR in June 1965 it set a world record for English Electric, for it contained the company's 2,000th diesel engine supplied to BR. No other railway ever had as many engines from one manufacturer.

Recalling their brief high speed exploits of June, D6881/2 were selected to celebrate the end of WR steam traction when a Farewell to Steam special was run on 27 November 1965. This circular tour from Paddington to Swindon, Bristol, Gloucester and Swindon, was hauled by Castle Class 4-6-0 7029 *Clun Castle,* with the final leg back to Paddington by diesel haulage at high-speed.

On 19 December 1965, following a landslip in the cutting on the Cardiff-Swansea main line just east of Bridgend, a derailment occurred when an empty stock train from Carmarthen to Bristol, headed by D1500 class No D1671, ran into the debris. The accident was made worse

The 14.37 Manchester Piccadilly-Harwich Parkeston Quay train at Sheffield Victoria in the charge of class 37 No 6968 on 3 January 1970, the last day that the train regularly travelled via Woodhead. *(Ian S. Carr)*

when almost immediately, D6983, heading an empty wagon train bound for Margam, ploughed into D1671. Both locomotives were very severely damaged, and subsequently scrapped. No D6983 was left at the adjacent scrapyard of R. S. Hayes Ltd, and was eventually officially removed from stock in September/October 1966.

Early 1966 saw WR D6700s working further afield to London and into the West Midlands and Merseyside, while speculation on their use on high-speed passenger work in multiple aroused by their appearances on Hereford-Paddington trains, and crew training at Old Oak Common, was again in the wind, but it proved not to be for mid-1966 marked the start of a mass transfer of D6700 class from the WR to the NER, and later to the Scottish and Eastern regions. About 100 locomotives were involved in changes during 1966/7. The WR resorted to using its 1700bhp diesel-hydraulics of D7000 class in West Wales on freight duties. The transfer saw many depots receiving D6700 for the first time, while in Scotland it was a type new to that region's diesel fleet. Here they went to Eastfield and Polmadie at Glasgow and to Haymarket, ringing the death-knell yet again for further medium-range steam classes. Haymarket soon put its allocation to work on the Waverley route, sharing freight duties with D200 and D1500 class units.

While the rumoured fast running with D6700 on the WR did not materialise, another example of their capability occurred on 16 May 1966 when a hurried replacement for the failed South Wales Pullman diesel-electric multiple-unit train resulted in D6881 hauling seven ordinary coaches of 238 tons tare from Cardiff to Paddington. The train covered the 113½ miles from Patchway to Paddington in 86min, at an average of 79mph, with the Badminton-Didcot part at an average of 90mph.

The practice of stabling D6700s at sub-depots in Wales is typified by this survey of July 1966

TABLE 13
MAIN DETAILS AND DIMENSIONS OF
D6700 CLASS, NOW CLASS 37

Details	Data
Axle layout	Co-Co
Engine model	12CSVT
Engine rating	1750BHP at 850rpm
Length over buffers	61ft 6in
Overall width	8ft 11 5/8 in
Overall height	12ft 10½in
Wheel diameter	3ft 7in
Bogie pivots	37ft 2in
Bogie wheelbase	13ft 6in
Total wheelbase	50ft 0in
Maximum speed	90mph
Continuous rail hp	1250
Maximum tractive effort	55,500 lb at 24.6% adhesion
Continuous tractive effort	35,000 lb at 13.6mph
Locomotive fuel capacity	830 glas
	950 gals including 120 gals auxiliary tank.
	980 gals
	1750 gals with boiler water tank converted to additional fuel tank.
Train heating boiler (when fitted)	Clayton RO2500 Mk I/II
Boiler water capacity	800 gals
Weight in working order depending on variations in installed equipment	101 tons 4 cwt to 105 tons 13 cwt

The inaugural molten-metal train from Cargo Fleet to Consett approaches South Pelaw on 4 August 1966 behind class 37s D6832 and D6712. The train comprised a dynamometer car and three torpedo wagons with barrier wagons. *(Ian S. Carr)*

The first of the class, D6700 poses for the camera with a Dagenham-Halewood Ford Motor Co train on 9 May 1963. *(British Railways)*

with the totals at main and sub-depots:

Pontypool Road	5
Aberbeeg	3
Ebbw Vale	2
Carmarthen	2
Whitland	1
Llanelly	4
Swansea East Dock	2
Landore	4
Neath (N & B)	3
Margam	2
Tondu	6
Rhymney	4
Cae Harris	3
Aberdare	4
Llantrisant	2
Barry	2
Radyr	11
Ebbw Jcn	12
Godfrey St	1
Severn Tunnel Jcn	3
Cardiff Canton	8

The reign of D6700s on the Lickey banking duties came to an end in October 1967 when a batch of D7000 diesel-hydraulics took over, releasing D6604/5/8 to Cardiff Canton. The D6700s nevertheless were to return early in 1973 when D7000 withdrawals made this necessary.

On the ER at Healey Mills depot a growing allocation of line-service diesels was building up to take over the steam workings of Wakefield, Mirfield, and Huddersfield sheds, and thus D6700s were seen frequently on both the L & Y and LNW lines to Lancashire. Ex-WR D6700s helped to finish steam on Wearside in September 1967, so ending the last outpost of pre-grouping steam power at Sunderland shed. A similar picture existed at Blyth where the new Cambois diesel depot with Gateshead D6700s took over the coal traffic from the Ashington area.

On the WR, South Wales units were working into Exeter in early 1968, the first normal service workings of this type here since the high speed runs of 1965. The loss of so many WR D6700s to the Scottish and Eastern regions meant that some rethinking had to be done on the WR which considered transferring those five portly and aptly-named diesel-hydraulics of the original Warship class, D600-4, to South Wales from Plymouth Laira. They were sent to Landore depot, Swansea, to release further D6700s employed on freight activities in the Pantyffynnon area. Only two were roused from their slumbers at Laira for the trials, soon being returned when they were unsuccessful.

Concurrently with air-brake trials on the Deltics at Derby Research Centre, Nos D6967/ were sent there in March 1968 on loan from

Renumbered No 37092, with its nose gangway doors removed, but retaining divided indicators, heads an empty wagon train at South Pelaw on 20 August 1974. *(Ian S. Carr)*

Stratford. Trials were run from Derby to Kettering and over the Peak Forest route. One of the Class 37 locomotives was used during April 1968 on a test programme for Westinghouse compressed air brakes over the Peak Forest 'mountain' route. A train of 99 ferry vans, the longest train ever run over BR, was worked to Peak Forest by the D6700 class and a D1500, the former working downhill from this point to Bakewell to test the brakes. The choice of this EE locomotive was made because, among other things, it had adequate compressor and reservoir capacity for such a long train. The tests were part of a UIC (International Railway Union) programme.

Other trials at this time involved D6700 itself, also from Stratford, which was push-and-pull fitted for Research Centre tests between Glasgow and Edinburgh during late February 1968. A BR standard corridor brake second No E34500 was equipped with a driving compartment, and four other coaches wired up with through control cables to allow D6700 to run propelling the train but controlled from the leading coach. On the tests, speeds of up to 90mph were achieved to gain data for the future introduction of push-pull working on this short Inter-City route to supersede diesel multiple-units. In the event BR opted for a form of push-pull working with Type 2 locomotives at both

ends of a six-coach train. The Scottish Region undertook further trials with D6700s in 1968, this time on the West Highland Line on passenger and freight as far as Fort William. Despite their power advantage over the 1160-1250bhp units normally used, again they were not permanently employed on this work.

An interesting NE area development was the use of D6700s on the new high-capacity molten-metal trains between Cargo Fleet, Tees-side and Consett Iron Works in the hills of central West Durham. This service was operated by special twin-articulated bogie wagons with a torpedo-shaped container. Three of these wagons, with spacers, formed a train, each wagon having a gross weight of 242 tons. After trials the first service train ran on 4 August 1969 with locomotives D6712 and D6791 and a dynamometer car, leaving Cargo Fleet at 12.30. Each car could carry 130 tons of metal in practice, but route axle-loading restrictions cut this to 100 tons. Classed as out of gauge an overall maximum of 20mph was placed on the train, with some sections as low as 5 or 10mph. After some initial problems the service operated for a period, two services operating daily from Tees-side at 0.610 and 18.30, and Consett at 13.20 and 01.22. The service was later discontinued. From 1969 to 1973 the WR Waterston-Birmingham (Albion) oil tank trains were booked for

While on loan to the BR Technical Centre at Derby, class 37 No D6968 was used on UIC air-brake equipment tests for Westinghouse, hauling trains of 99 BR ferry vans on the Derby-Kettering, Derby-Peak District routes in early 1968; they were the longest trains ever run on BR. *(Westinghouse Brake and Signal Co Ltd)*

D6700s in multiple pairs, while Tees-side units were similarly employed to Rowley Regis.

The decline of the WR diesel-hydraulic fleet hastened their elimination in West Wales from early 1972, and necessitated the provision of D6700s with train heating boilers for regular passenger operation, a duty almost unknown to the locomotives in that area. A modification to the class was the conversion of the train heating water tank, not required on locomotives without boilers, into a second fuel tank thereby extending their range and duration. This work was done at Cardiff Canton depot and the locomotives identified by a yellow spot under the number; the tanks were numbered 1 and 2.

An ER scheme to name some of the GE section locomotives after Eastern Counties Regiments faltered after only three locomotives—D6703/4/7—had been chosen. The names seemed pointless:

D6703   *First East Anglian Regiment*

D6704   *Second East Anglian Regiment*
D6707   *Third East Anglian Regiment*

The plates were fixed in the spring of 1963, but were always covered; the decision not to go ahead with names saw the plates removed without being publicly revealed by September 1963. Apart from the fact that naming was beginning to fall from favour at the highest BRB levels, planned rationalisation of military regiments would have invalidated some names. Moreover, it saved us from a host of unsuitable and monotonous names akin to the multitudes of Halls, Castles, Granges, etc, of GWR steam classes.

Other modifications to the Class 37 units include the sealing up of the nose gangway doors and at the time of writing some are fitted with the twin headlight system instead of the alpha-numerical roller blinds within their train identification panels, following the Deltics and the LM electric locomotives in this respect. Indeed as the newest of motive power has no provision for train reporting number displays clearly the abolition of the four-character head-codes on trains is in hand, even though the codes will continue in use on power signalbox control panels.

In common with other classes, individual

locomotive weights vary considerably, and may be summarised thus. Locomotives used on freight duties have their train-heating boilers removed so that with the locomotive air brake and vacuum train brake they weigh 100 tons 12 cwt or 103 tons 1 cwt with 950 gallons of fuel.

Dual braked examples—with straight air/ automatic air locomotive brakes, and automatic air/air-continuous vacuum train brakes weigh

101 tons 4 cwt and 103 tons 13 cwt with 950 gallons of fuel. Some WR locomotives have their redundant 800gall boiler water tank adapted as a second fuel tank, thereby raising total capacity to 1750gall.

When fitted with the Clayton R02500 Mk I/II boiler, the air/vacuum braked units weigh 102 tons 12 cwt while dual braked units weigh 103 tons 4 cwt or 105 tons 13 cwt.

TABLE 14

D6700 CLASS TYPE 3 — LATER BR CLASS 37

Original BR No	Works No VF or RSH	Works No Eng Elec	Date to Traffic	Reg New	Allocation Sep '75	Original BR No	Works No VF or RSH	Works No Eng Elec	Date to Traffic	Reg New	Allocation Sep '75
D6700	VF D579	2863	12/60	E	E	D6754	VF D708	3046	9/62	E	E
D6701	VF D580	2864	12/60	E	E	D6755	VF D709	3047	9/62	NE	E
D6702	VF D581	2865	12/60	E	E	D6756	VF D710	3048	9/62	NE	E
D6703	VF D582	2866	12/60	E	E	D6757	VF D711	3049	10/62	NE	E
D6704	VF D583	2867	1/61	E	E	D6758	VF D712	3050	10/62	NE	E
D6705	VF D584	2868	1/61	E	E	D6759	VF D713	3051	10/62	NE	E
D6706	VF D585	2869	1/61	E	E	D6760	VF D714	3052	10/62	NE	E
D6707	VF D586	2870	2/61	E	E	D6761	VF D715	3053	10/62	NE	E
D6708	VF D587	2871	2/61	E	E	D6762	VF D716	3054	10/62	NE	E
D6709	VF D588	2872	2/61	E	E	D6763	VF D717	3055	11/62	NE	E
D6710	VF D590	2874	2/61	E	E	D6764	VF D718	3056	11/62	NE	E
D6711	VF D591	2875	3/61	E	E	D6765	VF D719	3057	11/62	NE	E
D6712	VF D589	2873	3/61	E	E	D6766	VF D720	3058	11/62	NE	E
D6713	VF D592	2876	3/61	E	E	D6767	VF D721	3059	11/62	NE	E
D6714	VF D593	2877	3/61	E	E	D6768	VF D722	3060	11/62	NE	E
D6715	VF D594	2878	5/61	E	E	D6769	RSH 8315	3061	7/62	NE	E
D6716	VF D595	2879	6/61	E	E	D6770	RSH 8316	3062	8/62	NE	E
D6717	VF D596	2880	5/61	E	E	D6771	RSH 8317	3063	8/62	NE	E
D6718	VF D597	2881	6/61	E	E	D6772	RSH 8318	3064	9/62	NE	E
D6719	VF D598	2882	6/61	E	E	D6773	RSH 8319	3065	9/62	NE	E
D6720	VF D599	2883	6/61	E	E	D6774	RSH 8320	3066	9/62	NE	E
D6721	VF D600	2884	7/61	E	E	D6775	RSH 8321	3067	9/62	NE	E
D6722	VF D601	2885	7/61	E	E	D6776	RSH 8322	3068	10/62	NE	E
D6723	VF D602	2886	7/61	E	E	D6777	RSH 8323	3069	10/62	NE	E
D6724	VF D603	2887	8/61	E	E	D6778	RSH 8324	3070	10/62	NE	E
D6725	VF D604	2888	8/61	E	E	D6779	RSH 8325	3206	11/62	NE	E
D6726	VF D605	2889	9/61	E	E	D6780	RSH 8326	3207	11/62	NE	E
D6727	VF D606	2890	9/61	E	E	D6781	RSH 8327	3208	11/62	NE	E
D6728	VF D607	2891	9/61	E	E	D6782	RSH 8328	3029	11/62	NE	E
D6729	VF D608	2892	10/61	E	E	D6783	RSH 8329	3210	12/62	NE	E
D6730	VF D609	2893	10/61	NE	E	D6784	RSH 8330	3211	12/62	NE	E
D6731	VF D610	2894	10/61	NE	E	D6785	RSH 8331	3212	12/62	NE	E
D6732	VF D611	2895	3/62	NE	E	D6786	RSH 8332	3213	12/62	NE	E
D6733	VF D612	2896	3/62	NE	E	D6787	RSH 8333	3214	12/62	NE	E
D6734	VF D613	2897	3/62	NE	E	D6788	RSH 8334	3215	1/63	NE	E
D6735	VF D614	2898	4/62	NE	E	D6789	RSH 8335	3216	1/63	NE	E
D6736	VF D615	2899	4/62	NE	E	D6790	RSH 8336	3217	1/63	NE	E
D6737	VF D616	2900	5/62	NE	E	D6791	RSH 8337	3218	1/63	NE	E
D6738	VF D617	2901	5/62	NE	E	D6792	RSH 8338	3219	2/63	NE	E
D6739	VF D618	2902	5/62	NE	E	D6793	RSH 8339	3220	2/63	NE	E
D6740	VF D619	2903	6/62	NE	E	D6794	RSH 8341	3221	2/63	NE	E
D6741	VF D620	2904	6/62	NE	E	D6795	RSH 8342	3222	3/63	NE	E
D6742	VF D696	3034	6/62	E	E	D6796	VF D750	3225	11/62	E	E
D6743	VF D697	3035	6/62	E	E	D6797	VF D751	3226	12/62	E	E
D6744	VF D698	3036	6/62	E	E	D6798	VF D752	3227	12/62	E	E
D6745	VF D699	3037	7/62	E	E	D6799	VF D753	3228	12/62	E	E
D6746	VF D700	3038	7/62	E	E	D6800	VF D754	3229	12/62	E	E
D6747	VF D701	3039	7/62	E	E	D6801	VF D755	3230	12/62	E	E
D6748	VF D702	3040	8/62	E	E	D6802	VF D756	3231	1/63	E	E
D6749	VF D703	3041	8/62	E	E	D6803	VF D757	3232	1/63	E	E
D6750	VF D704	3042	8/62	E	E	D6804	VF D758	3233	1/63	E	E
D6751	VF D705	3043	8/62	E	E	D6805	VF D759	3234	1/63	E	E
D6752	VF D706	3044	9/62	E	E	D6806	VF D760	3235	1/63	E	E
D6753	VF D707	3045	9/62	E	E	D6807	VF D761	3236	1/63	E	E

Table 14 Cont.　D6700 Class Type 3 — Later BR Class 37

Original BR No	Works No VF or RSH	Works No Eng Elec	Date to Traffic	Reg New	Allocation Sep '75	Original BR No	Works No VF or RSH	Works No Eng Elec	Date to Traffic	Reg New	Allocation Sep '75
D6808	VF D762	3237	1/63	E	E	D6877	VF D841	3355	10/63	W	W
D6809	VF D763	3238	2/63	E	E	D6878	VF D842	3356	10/63	W	W
D6810	VF D764	3239	2/63	E	E	D6879	RSH 8400	3357	10/63	W	W
D6811	VF D765	3240	2/63	E	E	D6880	RSH 8401	3358	10/63	W	W
D6812	VF D766	3241	2/63	E	E	D6881	RSH 8402	3359	10/63	W	W
D6813	VF D767	3242	2/63	E	E	D6882	RSH 8403	3360	10/63	W	W
D6814	VF D768	3243	2/63	E	E	D6883	RSH 8404	3361	11/63	W	W
D6815	VF D769	3244	2/63	E	E	D6884	RSH 8405	3362	11/63	W	W
D6816	VF D770	3245	3/63	E	E	D6885	RSH 8406	3363	12/63	W	W
D6817	VF D771	3246	3/63	E	E	D6886	RSH 8407	3364	11/63	W	W
D6818	VF D772	3247	3/63	E	E	D6887	RSH 8408	3365	1/64	W	W
D6819	RSH 8379	3264	3/63	W	E	D6888	RSH 8409	3366	1/64	W	W
D6820	RSH 8380	3265	3/63	W	E	D6889	RSH 8410	3367	1/64	W	W
D6821	RSH 8381	3266	4/63	W	E	D6890	RSH 8411	3368	1/64	W	W
D6822	RSH 8382	3267	5/63	W	E	D6891	RSH 8412	3369	2/64	W	W
D6823	RSH 8383	3268	4/63	W	E	D6892	RSH 8413	3370	2/64	W	W
D6824	RSH 8384	3269	4/63	W	E	D6893	RSH 8414	3371	2/64	W	E
D6825	RSH 8385	3270	5/63	W	E	D6894	RSH 8415	3372	3/64	W	E
D6826	RSH 8386	3271	5/63	W	E	D6895	RSH 8416	3373	3/64	W	E
D6827	RSH 8387	3272	5/63	W	E	D6896	RSH 8417	3374	4/64	W	W
D6828	RSH 8388	3273	6/63	W	E	D6897	RSH 8418	3375	4/64	W	E
D6829	VF D803	3274	3/63	W	E	D6898	RSH 8419	3376	5/64	W	E
D6830	VF D804	3275	3/63	W	E	D6899	VF D843	3377	10/63	W	E
D6831	VF D805	3276	3/63	W	E	D6900	VF D844	3378	10/63	W	E
D6832	VF D806	3277	4/63	W	E	D6901	VF D845	3379	10/63	W	E
D6833	VF D807	3278	4/63	W	E	D6902	VF D846	3380	10/63	W	E
D6834	VF D808	3279	4/63	W	E	D6903	VF D847	3381	10/63	W	W
D6835	VF D809	3280	4/63	W	E	D6904	VF D848	3382	11/63	W	SC
D6836	VF D810	3281	4/63	W	E	D6905	VF D849	3383	11/63	W	SC
D6837	VF D811	3282	4/63	W	E	D6906	VF D850	3384	11/63	W	W
D6838	VF D812	3283	4/63	W	W	D6907	VF D851	3385	11/63	W	W
D6839	VF D813	3314	5/63	W	E	D6908	VF D852	3386	11/63	W	W
D6840	VF D814	3315	5/63	W	E	D6909	VF D853	3387	12/63	W	E
D6841	VF D815	3316	5/63	W	E	D6910	VF D854	3388	11/63	W	W
D6842	VF D816	3317	5/63	W	W	D6911	VF D855	3389	12/63	W	E
D6843	VF D817	3318	5/63	W	W	D6912	VF D856	3390	1/64	W	E
D6844	VF D818	3319	6/63	W	SC	D6913	VF D857	3391	1/64	W	W
D6845	VF D819	3320	6/63	W	SC	D6914	VF D858	3392	1/64	W	W
D6846	VF D820	3321	6/63	W	SC	D6915	VF D859	3393	1/64	W	E
D6847	VF D821	3322	6/63	W	SC	D6916	VF D860	3394	1/64	W	E
D6848	VF D822	3323	6/63	W	SC	D6917	VF D861	3395	1/64	W	W
D6849	VF D823	3324	6/63	W	SC	D6918	VF D862	3396	1/64	W	W
D6850	VF D824	3325	7/63	W	SC	D6919	VF D863	3405	1/64	W	E
D6851	VF D825	3326	7/63	W	SC	D6920	VF D864	3406	1/64	W	W
D6852	VF D826	3327	7/63	W	SC	D6921	VF D865	3407	1/64	W	E
D6853	VF D827	3328	7/63	W	SC	D6922	VF D866	3408	1/64	W	W
D6854	VF D828	3329	7/63	W	SC	D6923	VF D867	3409	2/64	W	W
D6855	VF D824	3330	7/63	W	SC	D6924	VF D868	3410	1/64	W	W
D6856	VF D830	3331	7/63	W	SC	D6925	VF D869	3411	2/64	W	W
D6857	VF D831	3332	7/63	W	SC	D6926	VF D870	3412	2/64	W	E
D6858	VF D832	3333	8/63	W	W	D6927	VF D871	3413	2/64	W	W
D6859	RSH 8390	3337	6/63	W	W	D6928	VF D872	3414	2/64	W	W
D6860	RSH 8391	3338	7/63	W	E	D6929	VF D873	3415	2/64	W	W
D6861	RSH 8392	3339	7/63	W	E	D6930	VF D874	3416	3/64	W	W
D6862	RSH 8393	3340	7/63	W	W	D6931	VF D875	3417	3/64	W	W
D6863	RSH 8394	3341	8/63	W	E	D6932	VF D876	3418	3/64	W	W
D6864	RSH 8395	3342	8/63	W	E	D6933	VF D877	3419	4/64	W	W
D6865	RSH 8396	3343	8/63	W	E	D6934	VF D878	3420	4/64	W	W
D6866	RSH 8397	3344	9/63	W	E	D6935	VF D879	3421	4/64	W	W
D6867	RSH 8398	3345	9/63	W	E	D6936	VF D880	3422	4/64	W	W
D6868	RSH 8399	3346	10/63	W	E	D6937	VF D881	3423	5/64	W	SC
D6869	VF D833	3347	8/63	W	E	D6938	VF D882	3424	6/64	W	E
D6870	VF D834	3348	8/63	W	E	D6939	VF D927	3496	8/64	W	W
D6871	VF D835	3349	9/63	W	E	D6940	VF D928	3497	8/64	W	W
D6872	VF D836	3350	9/63	W	E	D6941	VF D929	3498	9/64	W	W
D6873	VF D837	3351	9/63	W	E	D6942	VF D930	3499	9/64	W	E
D6874	VF D838	3352	9/63	W	E	D6943	VF D931	3500	9/64	W	W
D6875	VF D839	3353	9/63	W	W	D6944	VF D932	3501	9/64	W	W
D6876	VF D840	3354	10/63	W	W	D6945	VF D933	3502	10/64	W	E

The WR took delivery of the 300th class 37 for BR in October 1965. Here D6999, one of the class with cast-steel bogie frames, is seen on a coal train for Spencer Steelworks. (GEC Traction Ltd)

Original BR No	Works No VF or RSH	Works No Eng Elec	Date to Traffic	Reg New	Allo-cation Sep '75	Original BR No	Works No VF or RSH	Works No Eng Elec	Date to Traffic	Reg New	Allo-cation Sep '75
D6946	VF D934	3503	10/64	W	E	D6978	VF D967	3538	4/65	W	W
D6947	VF D935	3504	10/64	W	E	D6979	VF D968	3539	5/65	W	W
D6948	VF D936	3505	10/64	W	E	D6980	VF D969	3540	5/65	W	W
D6949	VF D937	3506	12/64	W	E	D6981	VF D970	3541	5/65	W	W
D6950	VF D938	3507	12/64	W	E	D6982	VF D971	3542	5/65	W	W
D6951	VF D939	3508	12/64	W	E	D6983	VF D972	3543	5/65	W	With-drawn
D6952	VF D940	3509	1/65	W	E						
D6953	VF D941	3510	1/65	W	W	D6984	VF D973	3544	5/65	W	W
D6954	VF D942	3511	1/65	W	W	D6985	VF D974	3545	5/65	W	W
D6955	VF D943	3512	1/65	W	W	D6986	VF D975	3546	6/65	W	W
D6956	VF D944	3513	1/65	W	W	D6987	VF D976	3547	6/65	W	W
D6957	VF D945	3514	1/65	W	W	D6988	VF D977	3548	6/65	W	W
D6958	VF D946	3515	1/65	W	W	D6989	VF D978	3549	6/65	W	W
D6959	VF D948	3519	1/65	E	E	D6990	VF D979	3550	6/65	W	W
D6960	VF D949	3520	1/65	E	E	D6991	VF D980	3551	6/65	W	W
D6961	VF D950	3521	1/65	E	E	D6992	VF D981	3552	7/65	W	W
D6962	VF D951	3522	1/65	E	E	D6993	VF D982	3553	7/65	W	W
D6963	VF D952	3523	1/65	E	E	D6994	VF D983	3554	7/65	W	W
D6964	VF D953	3524	1/65	E	E	D6995	VF D984	3555	7/65	W	W
D6965	VF D954	3525	2/65	E	E	D6996	VF D985	3556	7/65	W	W
D6966	VF D955	3526	2/65	E	E	D6997	VF D986	3557	7/65	W	W
D6967	VF D956	3527	2/65	E	E	D6998	VF D987	3558	8/65	W	W
D6968	VF D957	3528	2/65	E	E	D6999	VF D988	3559	8/65	W	W
D6969	VF D958	3529	2/65	W	W	D6600	VF D989	3560	8/65	W	W
D6970	VF D959	3530	3/65	W	W	D6601	VF D990	3561	9/65	W	W
D6971	VF D960	3531	3/65	W	W	D6602	VF D991	3562	9/65	W	W
D6972	VF D961	3532	3/65	W	W	D6603	VF D992	3563	9/65	W	W
D6973	VF D962	3533	4/65	W	W	D6604	VF D993	3564	9/65	W	W
D6974	VF D963	3534	4/65	W	W	D6605	VF D994	3565	10/65	W	W
D6975	VF D964	3535	4/65	W	W	D6606	VF D995	3566	10/65	W	W
D6976	VF D965	3536	4/65	W	W	D6607	VF D996	3567	10/65	W	W
D6977	VF D966	3537	4/65	W	W	D6608	VF D997	3568	11/65	W	W

CHAPTER 10

THE DELTICS OF THE EAST COAST ROUTE

Following the success of the prototype Deltic locomotive on BR an order was placed in early 1958 for 22 of these 3300bhp Co-Co machines for the heaviest and fastest East Coast passenger duties to replace 55 ex-LNER Pacific locomotives. Originally allocated running numbers D1000-21, then D1500-21, subsequently altered to D9000-21, they were noteworthy in being the only BR diesel locomotive class developed from a prototype which had the advantage of completing about 450,000 miles of running. Compared to the prototype, the production batch had an all-on weight of only 99 tons, a reversal of the usual result in which the developed unit was normally heavier than the prototype.

Certain important changes were made: the directly-driven 1500rpm main generators were replaced by a set of step-down gears between the engine and generator, reducing the armature speed to 1125rpm. The equipment layout was altered slightly and the superstructure construction, still on similar principles to the 1955 unit, was altered to present a different contour and appearance. Linear dimensions vary from the prototype, but they may be ascertained from the accompanying diagrams. The bogies were re-designed from experience gained with other BR English Electric diesel locomotives. The layout is double ended, arranged symmetrically each side of the train-heating boiler. The ER stipulated that the locomotives must be capable of very high yearly mileages, up to 220,000 miles a year, with a bogie change at half that distance. The BR Deltic fleet cost about £4 million, and took advantage of the offer of English Electric and Napier to take charge of maintenance, with the proviso that if the locomotives' mileages dropped below the contract figure, the sum paid by BR for maintenance would be reduced accordingly.

Although nominally of 3300bhp, a locomotive was produced with a continuous wheel-rim tractive effort amounting to 16 per cent adhesion at 32.5 per cent of the top speed. When studied, this corresponded to a 35,000lb tractive effort at 32.5mph, equivalent to 83 per cent transmission efficiency or 3000 rail horse power, giving a generator input of 3600hp, and leaving nothing for the auxiliaries with the engines operating at their rated horse power. At 99 tons the production Deltics had a power-weight ratio of 67 lb per bhp, or 33.3bhp per ton.

The mechanical structure followed generally that of the prototype Deltic, based on an under-frame of four main longitudinals, the inner being fabricated by welding steel plate to form flanged girders and stiffened by using deep section between the bogies; the outer ones were fabricated from rolled steel channels. Bracing was introduced by cross-members. The top flange is swept down between the bogies to lower the engine room floor level and the whole is decked with oil-tight welded steel plate with a dished area underneath to provide a drainage pan and sump clearance.

The bogies, identical to those fitted to the D6700 and D400 classes, are interesting in that they differ from those of the prototype Deltic by the removal of cross-laminated springs of swing bolster type and the substitution of coil springs. This modification was first applied to the D6700s whose bogies were developed from those of the prototype Deltic, the resulting bogie being applied to the BR Deltics.

The whole superstructure, like the prototype, formed one load bearing carrying unit of steel, fabricated by welding. Bodyside ventilation is by sliding window units, with light alloy removable roof sections over the power units housing water and oil cooling groups. They comprise resiliently mounted radiator, header tank, fan, pipe runs, and thermostats, all removable as one unit. Hinged access doors above and below the equipment are also provided. There is a similar removable section over the train-heating boiler.

The engine-generator sets are arranged with the generators at the outer ends adjacent to the switch gear cubicle forming the inner bulkhead of the adjoining cab. Between the engines was the train-heating boiler, a Spanner Mk II unit with a capacity of 2000 lb per hour, since removed on fitting of electric train-heating equipment. Above the boiler area is an asbestos lagged stainless steel cylindrical exhaust silencer for each engine. Battery boxes are arranged centrally between the engines on the inner bodyside.

Four interconnected alloy fuel tanks of

900gals capacity are flexibly suspended from the underframe. Fuelling is by flight-type nozzles or by pressure hose; water was taken in by bodyside chutes or originally by water pick-up scoops from track water troughs, since removed with the abandonment of troughs after the end of steam.

Lubricating oil and engine coolant supply tanks are placed between the inner and outer underframe members. Side access doors on the inner cab-bulkhead and walkways give access to the power units.

In front of each cab is a high bulbous nose unit, one containing two vacuum exhausters, the other the air-compressor. Also fitted is a water-flush toilet and wash basin. Both nose units contain a Keith-Blackman traction motor blower, air reservoirs and fire extinguishers.

In order to give good visibility over the high nose units the cab floors were raised by a plinth.

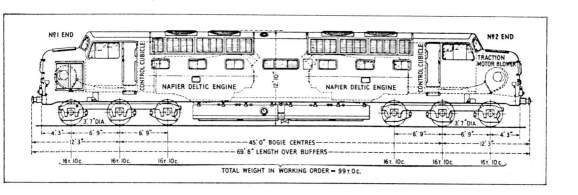

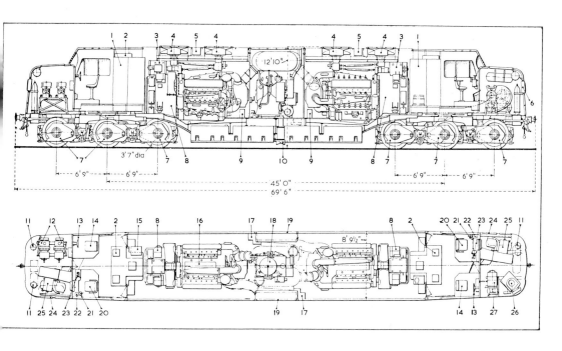

Fig 12: Layout diagram of BR class 55 Deltic locomotive comparison with Fig 7 is interesting. Key: 1 Control equipment cubicle; 2 Resistors; 3 Auxiliary generators; 4 Cooling fan; 5 Header tank, water system; 6 Route indicator; 7 Traction motor; 8 Main generator; 9 Lubricating oil tank; 10 Water pick up; 11 Fire extinguisher — CO_2; 12 Brake exhauster; 13 Handbrake; 14 Assistant driver's seat; 15 Cooker; 16 Deltic engine; 17 Water tank filling duct; 18 Train heating boiler; 19 Engine air-filters; 20 Driver's seat; 21 Airbrake valve; 22 Vacuum brake valve; 23 Controller; 24 Traction — motor air filters; 25 Traction motor blower; 26 Toilet; 27 Air compressor; *(Author's collection)*

The up Flying Scotsman passing Manors station, Newcastle behind Deltic No D9019 (unnamed) on 1 August 1964. *(Ian S. Carr)*

The driver's controls are conventionally arranged with air and vacuum brake controls to the left, power controller and reverser to the right of the desk; the usual lights and instrumentation together with deadman's treadle are provided. Locomotive air brakes are supplied by the Worthington-Simpson two-stage compressor, and train vacuum was by a pair of Reavell exhausters. Compressed-air sanding is fitted.

The engines are a pair of Napier Deltic D18-25, 18 cylinder units, each rated at 1650bhp at 1500rpm. Their three banks of cylinders are arranged in the form of an equilateral triangle.

As mentioned earlier, the Deltic was nominally capable of much higher than its rated power. The fuel pumps were set to UIC 10 per cent maximum overload, the extra being used to good effect with train loads of about 400 tons. In favourable wind, and with allowance for train rolling resistance and gradients, a Deltic was able to give 2500dbhp or, allowing for the locomotive weight, 3200hp, or with a small allowance for auxiliaries about 3800hp, about 15 per cent higher than the figure normally quoted for this class. Mention of favourable wind is not so

frivolent as might be imagined for a strong head/cross wind, for example south-westerly gales reacting against up East Coast expresses on exposed sections of line, can consume a considerable amount of power from the locomotives and effectively boost power if trains have a following tail wind.

The English Electric type 829 main generators are flange-mounted six-pole single-bearing dc machines with six interpoles and a compensating winding. The main poles have separately-excited winding with the usual series winding for engine starting. At the drive end the armature shaft is supported in the engine final drive bearing and at the commutator end in a self-aligning roller bearing. Ventilation for the generator is by a fan mounted at the drive end.

Both generators are connected in series, each having a continuous rating of 1650amp, 660V; maxima of 2100-2400amps are available for up to one minute at starting a train, provided the locomotive moves within three seconds. Currents of 1800-2100amp may be used for up to five minutes. The control system provides for single engine operation at full tractive effort but at reduced speeds.

The centenary of the Flying Scotsman; a Deltic takes the northbound train across Welwyn viaduct on 13 April 1962. *(British Railways)*

The saddle-mounted auxiliary generators are driven by gearing from the engine phasing gears at 1.67 times engine speed. They have a 45kW output, tension being held at 110V through the whole engine speed range. Current for engine starting, by excitation of main generators, is shared by the auxiliary generators, except for single-engine operation.

The six English Electric type 538 nose-suspended traction motors are axle-hung and rated at 400hp each at 533amp, 600V. They are four-pole series-wound force-ventilated machines with two stage automatic field weakening to extend the locomotive power/speed range to their full extent. The reduction gear ratio is 21:59.

The adoption of electric train-heating by BR saw the class fitted for this requirement by tapping the traction generators; the locomotives were thus fitted for both steam and electric heating.

The Deltics were delivered to all three recipient depots, Finsbury Park, ER; Gateshead, NER; and Haymarket, ScR, in turn so that crew training and trial running could be carried out simultaneously. D9001 was first to be delivered, arriving at Doncaster works for acceptance tests on 16 January 1961; it went light to Stratford for the day on the 18th, returning the same day. D9000 and D9002 arrived at Doncaster from Vulcan Foundry in late February and early March respectively.

Trials with D9001 on the GN section included 100mph running down Stoke bank. It was finally allocated to Finsbury Park on 6 March. Initial duties for D9001 included crew training and then parcels trains to Doncaster and back, followed by passenger trains on the same route. D9000 arrived in the London area in early March, and amongst its initial workings was a 14 coach test train between New Southgate and Doncaster on 15 March.

More interesting was D9001's exploit the same day with an 11 coach dynamometer test train of 385 tons which ran from Kings Cross to Newark, 120 miles in 93min. Doncaster, 156½ miles, was reached in 125min. The first run to Newcastle, on the 21st, saw the 385 ton load run from Kings Cross to Newcastle, with a 2min stop at Darlington, in 253min for the 232 miles, Grantham being passed at 08.27, Doncaster 09.13½, and York at 09.44.

Of signalling interest in connection with the Deltic trials was the use of double-section block working with the 4-pause-4 bell code used for the Coronation and Silver Jubilee trains of pre-war years. An extensive signal modification programme entailing the moving out of distant signals to give adequate braking distance for 100mph running was put in hand on the East Coast route to permit the full potential of the Deltics to be realised.

D9000 arrived at Haymarket on 21 March 1961 and Gateshead received D9002 the following day. The final allocations were to be eight Deltics each at Finsbury Park and Haymarket and six at Gateshead, which has rarely been varied. With one at each depot, Finsbury Park put theirs on the 08.20 Kings Cross-Hull as far as Doncaster; Gateshead based theirs at South Gosforth diesel depot for crew training, then used it on parcels trains between Newcastle and Carlisle; Haymarket meanwhile based theirs at Leith Central diesel depot for crew training, and training trains to Berwick.

Some troubles with fractured bogie frames held up deliveries in April, and the first few units were returned to their maker's works for attention. This delay was necessary to allow D6700 class locomotives from the GE section

TABLE 15
MAIN DETAILS AND DIMENSIONS OF
D9000 CLASS DELTIC LOCOMOTIVES, NOW CLASS 55

Description	Data
Axle layout	Co-Co
Engine model	Two engines D18-25
Engine rating	1650BHP at 1500rpm each
Locomotive weight, in working order	99 tons 0cwt
Locomotive weight, empty	94 tons 8cwt
Brakes, locomotive	Straight air/Automatic air
Brakes, train	Automatic air/Air continuous vacuum
Train heating	Spanner Mk II boiler and Electric from main generators.
Boiler water supply	830gals
Length over buffers	69ft 6in
Overall width	8ft 9½in
Overall height	12ft 11in
Wheel diameter	3ft 7in
Bogie pivots	45ft 0in
Bogie wheelbase	13ft 6in
Total wheelbase	58ft 0in
Maximum tractive effort	500,000 lb at 21.7% adhesion
Continuous tractive effort	30,500 lb at 32.5mph
Continuous rail hp	2640
Locomotive and boiler fuel capacity	826 gals

D9007, *Pinza*, first of the class to be named, at Sunderland with the 12.00 Newcastle-Colchester/Kings Cross train on 17 July 1967. The locomotive is fitted with specially tuned warning horns located inside the nose. *(Ian S. Carr)*

priority in bogie modifications in time for their commitment in the summer timetable.

In May, D9003 was exhibited at Marylebone Parcels Depot from the 11th to the 14th, together with other rolling stock, to mark the Golden Jubilee of the Institution of Locomotive Engineers. Deliveries proceeded slowly, giving the ageing LNER Pacifics a reprieve. Moreover it had not gone unnoticed that as the Deltics had no provision to exchange crews, because there were no gangways, Deltic haulage of the Flying Scotsman/Elizabethan would bring to an end East Coast Kings Cross-Edinburgh non-stop running.

During the summer/autumn of 1961 the Deltics had a poor spell, but many individual examples of good running occurred. The engine makers stated that the difficulties occurred because of their failure to test and examine a production engine thoroughly before use in the locomotives. As it happened, a large number of engines had been delivered to Vulcan Foundry before the test engine had been stripped down. An early fault on the production engines was the discovery of fretting wear on the splined output shafts, this coming to notice on the test engine at 1000 hours. Fortunately this problem *was* dealt with prior to installation of the engines in the locomotives.

Troubles with cylinder liner corrosion were overcome by using a coolant water additive, while cracking in the welds of the engine exhaust-drum tank was eventually overcome by redesign following temporary attention. The engine shut-down gear, an automatic valve which shut down the engines in emergencies, gave trouble by being over-sensitive to vibration, resulting in shut-down when no emergency existed. Cracking of close-forged connecting rods in two engines and the quick replacement of the rods in the rest saved the engines from possibility of large scale failures. Corrosion fatigue resulting in cylinder liner fractures was overcome by stronger liners. Piston modifications following cases of loose piston crowns in 1961 resulted in redesign and, together with the aforementioned liner troubles, was expected to continue into 1962, but to be remedied once the new components were ready.

The second 12 months of Deltic service, August 1962 to August 1963, saw some failings of coolant-pump drives, while the 'expected problems' resulted in five engines developing loose piston crowns and three failing because of cracked cylinder liners.

Nevertheless, the Deltic engines in the locomotives achieved an average of 97 per cent of their gross possible running hours between overhaul. The process of quick engine replacement, an eight hour operation, helped to maintain high availability and, according to Napiers, justified entirely the repair by replacement technique. The availability of the Deltic locomotives was 80 per cent in 1961/62 and 88½ per cent in 1962/3. The modified engines in their final form gave little trouble and put their locomotives into the world-beater class.

During 1961 a naming policy was evolved by the ER for its Deltics, being subsequently followed by the NE and Scottish regions. The naming themes selected were hardly original, the ER continuing an LNER practice by adopting racehorse names as in their previous A1, A2, A3 Pacifics, while both the NE and Scottish regions applied dreary regimental names.

Naming of the ER examples was done without fuss at Doncaster works, but the others in most cases were involved in ceremonies which in some cases were at locations way off the locomotives'

normal route. D9004 was named at Inverness, D9010 at Dumfries, D9021 at Stirling, etc. The last locomotive was not named until September 1965.

By March 1962 with the delivery of D9021 the 22 Deltics were allocated as follows:

Finsbury Park	D9001/3/7/9/12/15/18/20
Gateshead	D9002/5/8/11/14/17
Haymarket	D9000/4/6/10/13/16/19 /21

In the early part of 1962 the class made a number of visits to the works of Robert Stephenson & Hawthorns at Darlington in connection with the aforementioned troubles but improving availability saw the Deltics working most of their diagrams by mid 1962, putting in good mileages. The modifications and advice of the Napier and English Electric technicians proved its worth. With their stipulated contract mileage of 220,000 miles per year, or 331 days available for traffic, the cost of keeping the Deltics tuned to the pitch required for their arduous duties was high.

The question of how many Deltic engines are kept as spares in the exchange pool, how often engines are changed, and what are the labour costs involved, have never been satisfactorily answered. Estimates of how many spare main components exist have been put at around a dozen engines and generators and six bogies. It must be said that even if they were not attaining full contract mileages, any locomotive achieving mileages like the Deltics could probably more than substantiate costs. During their first service year aggregate totals were 2,750,000 miles, with a total fleet mileage at the end of 1964 of 11,645,000 miles.

The BR requirement that the Deltics could under no circumstances be out of service during the summer timetables saw them cover over one million miles during the twelve weeks of the 1963 summer. On rare occasions the class were seen in multiple on the main line, while other times saw them visiting places off their normal routes, like Sheffield, Cambridge, Bradford, Scarborough, etc.

With the start of the 1966 summer timetable on 18 April, trains diagrammed for Deltic haulage were booked to cover some sections at maximum speeds of 100mph. Trains from Kings Cross to Leeds were timed overall at an average of 70mph, taking 160min, while Bradford was to be reached in 184min, the fastest ever on these routes. The Flying Scotsman was booked to run the 393 miles between London and Edinburgh in 350min, an average of 67.3mph, again the fastest ever.

In preparation for this speed-up a high-speed demonstration run for the press was arranged for 10 April. D9012 hauled the train of eight coaches weighing 286 tons, departing Kings Cross at 09.56, arriving Doncaster at 12.02. The return trip left at 13.56, arriving Kings Cross at 16.04. From this it was patently obvious that the Deltics were far superior to anything before or, as yet, since on the East Coast Route.

The first five year maintenance contract ended in 1966, at which point the Deltic engines were reaching 5000-6000 hours running; and the next contract was based on a 5000-5500 hours engine running. The maintenance schedules were briefly an A examination every 24 hours at layover times, B every seven days, at longer layovers or weekends; C and D were at 28 and 84 days operation, and together with Doncaster works visits were covered by the spare locomotives of the fleet, which usually stood at five locomotives with 17 or 18 in traffic. Even though these engine-hour periods were stipulated and adhered to, some engines had achieved 8000-10,000 hour life.

The decision to fit electric train heating as standard on new BR rolling stock to overcome the perennial steam generator troubles which accounted for so large a proportion of diesel

Diverted via Carlisle and the Waverley route because of a derailment on its normal route near Acklington on Sunday, 17 July 1967, Deltic No 9017, *The Durham Light Infantry*, enters the Border City with the 10.00 from Edinburgh to Kings Cross. *(Ian S. Carr)*

locomotive defects, meant that such new stock would be first used on more important trains. As a result the Deltics were converted to electric train heating (ETH) from early 1967, D9007 being first.

The 1967 summer timetables, recast from 6 March giving very intensive diagrams with maximum Deltic locomotive usage, eliminated spare Deltics held at each allocated depot; 18 locomotives were diagrammed, six from each depot.

On the Darlington-York race track the Deltics put up quite remarkable high speed running with a consistency so common as to be repetitive. The number of logs published with speed in the 100mph range have been many: the writer timed one in early 1966 with D9006 on the up Heart of Midlothian hauling 490 tons. It covered the 21.1 miles from Otterington to Beningborough in 12min 47 seconds. Speeds of 97-101 were recorded at Danby Wiske, 10.4 miles from Darlington, Otterington, 17.6 miles, Thirsk, 21.9 miles, Tollerton, 34.4 miles, and Beningborough, 38.6 miles. The time for the 44.1 miles run was 31min 55sec in spite of PW slacks at Wiske Moore troughs and Skelton Junction about two miles from York. At no time over the Eryholme-Beningborough section did speed fall below 79mph. By the end of 1967 Deltics had covered 22½ million miles.

Apart from the seven month transfer of D9021 from Haymarket to Finsbury Park in November 1964, few transfers have occurred. The largest move, again of about seven months' duration, was in November 1967 when D9001/3/9 went north to Haymarket and D9000/16/19 came south as part of a plan to concentrate all air-brake fitted units at Finsbury Park. At this time air-braking was being adopted by BR, and a number of test runs with air braked stock were underway, D9016, for example in October/November 1967 with 16 coaches between London and Edinburgh. For the same purpose D9013 was on loan to the BR Research Department, Derby in early 1968. By the end of April 1968 16 Deltics had air-brake equipment and the exchange of locomotives to correct the allocation concerning D9000/1/3/9/12/13/16/19 took place in June.

In 1970 high speed tests were conducted on the LMR electrified section between Tring and Leighton Buzzard involving Deltic D9020, electric locomotives, and electric multiple-units to assess the effects of trains passing each other at speeds over 100mph, one of the rare occasions a Deltic was away from exclusive use on the East Coast route.

Their only scheduled running on unfamiliar routes has usually been due to diversions; for example, following derailments between New-castle and Edinburgh Deltics have been diverted via Carlisle on Anglo-Scottish duties. Initially this involved running on the Waverley route from Carlisle to Edinburgh, but since closure, via Carstairs.

TABLE 16
D9000 "DELTIC" CLASS TYPE 5 — LATER
BR CLASS 55

Original BR No	Works No Vulcan Wks	Works No Eng Elec	Date to Traffic	Reg Allocation, new and at 31.10.75	
D9000	D557	2905	P3/61	SC	SC
D9001	D558	2906	2/61	E	E
D9002	D559	2907	2/61	NE	E
D9003	D560	2908	3/61	E	E
D9004	D561	2909	P4/61	SC	SC
D9005	D562	2910	5/61	NE	E
D9006	D563	2911	P7/61	SC	SC
D9007	D564	2912	6/61	E	E
D9008	D565	2913	7/61	NE	E
D9009	D566	2914	7/61	E	E
D9010	D567	2915	P8/61	SC	SC
D9011	D568	2916	8/61	NE	E
D9012	D569	2917	9/61	E	E
D9013	D570	2918	P10/61	SC	SC
D9014	D571	2919	9/61	NE	E
D9015	D572	2920	10/61	E	E
D9016	D573	2921	P11/61	SC	SC
D9017	D574	2922	11/61	NE	E
D9018	D575	2923	11/61	E	E
D9019	D576	2924	P13/61	SC	SC
D9020	D577	2925	2/62	E	E
D9021	D578	2926	P5/62	SC	E

TABLE 17
LIST OF NAMES CARRIED BY
D9000 DELTIC CLASS LOCOMOTIVES

The month of naming, either at special ceremonies or at visits to works, is given.

Locomotive Name	Date Named	Name
D9000	18/6/62	Royal Scots Grey
D9001	7/61	St Paddy
D9002	4/4/63	The King's Own York-shire Light Infantry
D9003	7/61	Meld
D9004	23/5/64	Queen's Own Highlander
D9005	8/10/63	The Prince of Wales's Own Regiment of Yorkshire
D9006	5/12/64	The Fife and Forfar Yeomanry
D9007	6/61	Pinza
D9008	30/9/64	The Green Howards
D9009	8/61	Alycidon
D9010	8/5/65	The King's Own Scottish Borderer
D9011	28/5/63	The Royal Northumber-land Fusiliers
D9012	9/61	Crepello
D9013	16/1/63	The Black Watch
D9014	20/10/63	The Duke of Wellington's Regiment
D9015	10/61	Tulyar
D9016	28/7/64	Gordon Highlander
D9017	29/10/63	The Durham Light Infantry
D9018	12/61	Ballymoss
D9019	11/9/65	Royal Highland Fusilier
D9020	2/62	Nimbus
D9021	29/11/63	Argyll and Sutherland Highlander

TABLE 18

OFFICIAL RECORD OF INDIVIDUAL DELTIC PERFORMANCE AUGUST 1962–SEPTEMBER 1963

Locomotive Number	One Year's Mileage	Service Hours	Days available for Traffic	Availability (Percentage)
9000	158,459	3652	299	82
9001	167,942	3338	276	75.5
9002	130,187	2534	265	72.7
9003	186.502	3708	313	85.5
9004	184,160	3053	316	86.8
9005	130,976	2663	273	74.8
9006	182,670	3068	309	84.5
9007	187,130	3644	293	80.4
9008	151,193	2970	291	80
9009	170,138	3431	300	82.1
9010	186,138	3184	299	82
9011	138.186	2682	278	76.1
9012	160,155	3250	280	76.8
9013	168,334	2711	286	78.5
9014	135,968	2695	272	74.7
9015	180,135	3612	280	76.8
9016	182,456	3019	301	82.4
9017	151,379	2965	295	80.8
9018	163,745	3320	305	83.7
9019	186,775	3114	302	82.9
9020	180,025	3611	300	82.1
9021	187,167	3289	316	86.8

The 1970/1 timetables brought further speed-ups, made possible by the removal of long-standing speed restrictions by track improvements, such as those at Offord where curves with limits of 70mph were straightened by filling in part of the River Ouse, raising the speed limit to 100mph. Track slewing at Grantham, Durham, Newton Hall, etc, were similar cases, and a year or so later the severe 15mph for all trains through the tortuous curves of Peterborough was eliminated by the building of a new platform and through lines on an almost straight alignment.

Two trains each way Kings Cross-Newcastle were timed to cover the 268½ miles in 215min, saving 15min on previous running, while Leeds was brought only to within 159min from Kings Cross, inclusive of a stop at Wakefield. Between 1958 and 1970 the best Kings Cross-Newcastle timings were:

Year	Type of Traction	Time
1958	Steam	5hrs 00min

Above: Diverted via Leamside (old main line), D9009, *Alycidon*, with experimental headcode panel, heads the 10.35 Newcastle-Kings Cross at Penshaw North, Sunday, 3 June 1973. *(Ian S. Carr)*

Left: Renumbered Deltic No 55019, *Royal Highland Fusilier*, approaches Relly Mill with the 11.00 Kings Cross-Newcastle on 14 September 1974. The new alignment of the East Coast main line is under construction on the right. *(Ian S. Carr)*

1961	Steam	4hrs 30min
1964	Deltic Diesel	4hrs 00min
1967	Deltic Diesel	3hrs 50min
1970	Deltic Diesel	3hrs 35min

During the 1930s there was of course the 4 hour schedule between Kings Cross and Newcastle by the Silver Jubilee and Coronation trains but with lighter loads than those of postwar years. By 1974 the Deltic-hauled Newcastle Executive was running the 268½ miles in 3hrs 32min, including a 2min stop at Darlington.

During late 1972 D9009 was fitted with twin headlights at both ends inside the train indicator panel replacing the two outer digits, other examples being equipped later.

On 16 January 1973 D9010 achieved the honour of being the first British diesel-electric locomotive to reach two million miles since it entered service in July 1961. This was achieved in record time, 12 years, and was followed in the following two months by others of the class with similar mileages.

Early in 1975 two Deltics were again used for trials away from the East Coast main line, this time under the direction of the BR Derby Research Centre over the Reading-Foxhall section of the WR main line through Didcot, to test permissible dynamic track loadings. Two Deltics, Nos 55001/7, were selected for tests on 12/19 January conducted in association with trial running by the prototype High Speed Train over dipped rail joints. Dipped rail joints, that is, joints not maintained absolutely level which allow the passing wheels of trains to drop, are a constant problem to railway engineers and more so as speeds increase, although only where jointed, as distinct from continuous welded, track survives. Deltics were chosen because BR limits for rail and formation stresses are based on locomotives running at 100mph.

The success of the high-speed Deltic-hauled East Coast services is remarkable considering the age of these hardworking locomotives, some approaching 15 years of age by the end of 1975. At the time of writing it would appear likely that 1975/6 would see these World-beating locomotives start to reach individual mileages of over 2,200,000 miles, with a fleet mileage of almost 48 million miles. With their scheduled replacement by the HST in 1978 on the East Coast route, let us hope that the idea to use them to speed up some of the East Coast shorter distance expresses proves true.

We now only have to consider the 1966 proposal of English Electric Traction Division and G. F. Fiennes of the ER board for a Super-Deltic, which would have been a very interesting locomotive indeed. Based on the D400 or class

50 mechanical portion, with its Co-Co axle-layout and a total service weight of 114 tons, it would have had a 19 tons axle-load within the maximum permitted on BR. It was to be powered by a pair of Napier Deltic T18-27K engines developed from those of the BR Deltic locomotives, each engine producing 2200bhp. Each was to drive an English Electric type 841 main generator, thus giving a 4400bhp locomotive. Since 1967, further Deltic engine development of the 18-cylinder engine could now provide a 5300bhp locomotive using two CT18-52K engines. It is a great pity that these proposals never materialised, for, following the success of the 3300bhp locomotives, there seems no doubt at all that the Super-Deltic would have been quite remarkable.

TABLE 19
MAIN DETAILS AND DIMENSIONS OF PROPOSED SUPER DELTIC LOCOMOTIVE OF 1966

Description	Data
Axle layout	Co-Co
Engine model	Two engines, T18-27K
Engine rating	2200BHP at 1600rpm, each
Locomotive weight, in working order	114 tons
Brakes	Independent air/Automatic air
Train heating	Electric from main generator
Length over body	67ft 6in
Overall width	8ft 9½in
Overall height	12ft 9 1/16 in
Wheel diameter	3ft 9in
Bogie pivots	42ft 4in
Bogie wheelbase	14ft 9in

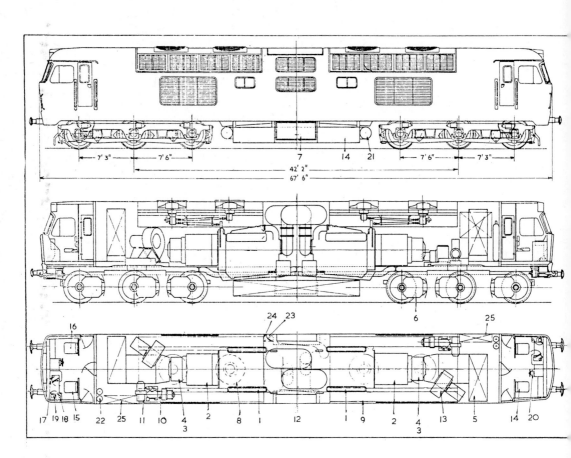

Fig 13: Layout of proposed 'Super-Deltic' locomotive of 1966, for East Coast route services of BR. Based on a class 50 mechanical structure, it would have had two Napier Deltic 2200bhp engines. Key: 1 Engine, Napier Deltic 18; 2 Main generator; 3 Train heating generator; 4 Auxiliary alternator; 5 Control cubicle; 6 Traction motor; 7 Battery; 8 Radiator fan; 9 Radiator; 10 Compressor; 11 Exhauster; 12 Silencer; 13 Traction motor blower; 14 Fuel tank; 15 Driver's seat; 16 Assistant's seat; 17 Master controller; 18 Air brake valve (ind); 19 Auto air brake valve; 20 Handbrake; 21 Air reservoirs; 22 CO_2 bottles; 23 Urinal; 24 Water tank; 25 Brake equipment frame. *(GEC Traction Ltd)*

CHAPTER 11

DP2: A REMARKABLE PROTOTYPE

The years 1961/2 saw BR searching for a suitable design to provide the basis of their second generation Type 4 diesel-electrics, capable of employment on forthcoming accelerated services at speeds of 100mph, beyond the capacity of existing locomotives in the Type 4 category. The almost simultaneous decision by three British locomotive manufacturers to construct locomotives in prototype form in the 2700-2800bhp range, carried on six axles, provided some stimulating work. Three excellent prototypes resulted, and ran for considerable mileages on BR.

The prototype locomotives were: a twin-engined 2800bhp unit by Brush Traction named *Falcon*; a 2750bhp machine by Birmingham Railway Carriage and Wagon Co Ltd,-Sulzer Bros (London) Ltd,-Associated Electrical Industries, named *Lion*; and, finally, English Electric's 2700bhp unit No DP2. Of these, the first two had continental diesel engines, admittedly built under licence in the UK and highlighted one of those strange facets of BR dieselisation—the use of such engines when British ones were available.

The outcome of the prototypes is garbled, for even while they were running, BR had ordered 20 of the D1500 class from Brush. This class owed little to the Brush *Falcon* unit with its high-speed Maybach engines, but was rather more akin to its Sulzer-powered competitor, *Lion*, for it made use of the same engine, largely because BR had 20 sets on hand. The D1500s were eventually constructed to a total of 512 units, but the problems which have occurred with these locomotives, standard though they are, is well known, and has been covered fully in the technical press. Nevertheless, the wheel has turned full circle, and the final batch of Type 4 diesel-electrics for BR were based on these prototypes, but with the flat front layout of both *Falcon* and *Lion*, but the innards of the amazing English Electric locomotive DP2, our subject here.

The mechanical portion of DP2 conformed closely to that of the production Deltics of 1960/1, described in Chapter 10. The layout of DP2 comprised the cooling group arranged behind No 1 cab at the free end of the engine,

balanced at the other end by the Clayton RO2000 train heating boiler; the Deltics had these items placed centrally. The boiler was in the engine room, but the cooling group was in its own compartment with sliding doors.

No 1 nose housed two Reavell FRU type exhausters, electrically driven by flange-mounted motors, and the blower for No 1 end bogie traction motor ventilation. The second nose housed No 2 traction motor blower and a Worthington-Simpson electrically-driven compressor.

Cab layouts were identical, with standard left-hand drive and a second man's seat on the right. Control equipment was housed in two cubicles forming the rear bulkhead walls of the cabs between the doors. Air for the engine room was admitted through wall-mounted, panel-type, oil-wetted metal filters, internally mounted along the engine room walls below cantrail level. Air for the auxiliaries was admitted through similar filters behind grilles in the left hand side of each nose compartment.

Batteries, in glass fibre containers, were under tread plates in the radiator compartment, while fuel tanks and boiler feed water tanks were flexibly slung from the underframe, being of light alloy fabrications. Frost insulation and steam coil heating were provided for the water tanks.

Train braking was by vacuum, and for the locomotive by straight-air brake; a deadman's circuit, activated by a pedal, was fitted at the driver's seat. Instrumentation comprised warning lights, wheel slip detector, and the usual controls. The bogies were the same as fitted to the D6700 and BR Deltic classes.

The engine comprised the first traction application of the English Electric 16 CSVT direct-injection pressure-charged and inter-cooled vee engine in its 2700bhp form, running at 850rpm. Four Napier pressure-chargers, two for each bank of cylinders, were fitted, being exhaust gas-turbine units.

Radiator panels in pairs, one behind the other, were fitted on both sides of the locomotive. The outer panels were interconnected and circulated the coolant from the charge-air-cooling circuit; the inner ones cooled

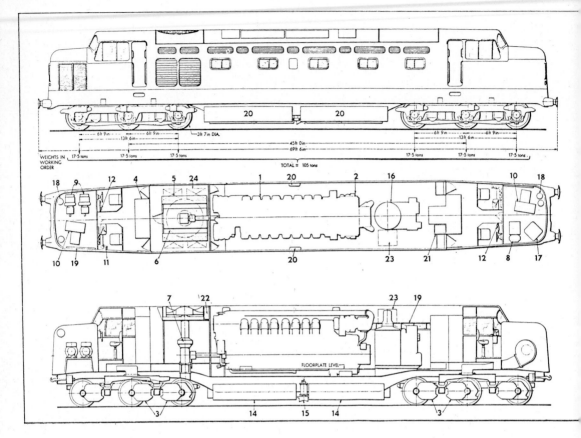

Fig 14: Diagram of the English Electric built and owned prototype 2700bhp Co-Co diesel-electric No DP2 built in 1961. Key: 1 E.E. 16 CSVT 2700bhp diesel engine; 2 Main generator; 3 Traction motor; 4 No 1 equipment frame; 5 Radiator panels; 6 Radiator fan; 7 Magnetic coupling; 8 Air compressor; 9 Vacuum exhausters; 10 Traction motor blower; 11 Driver's brake valves; 12 Hotplate; 14 Water tank; 15 Water scoop; 16 Train heating boiler; 17 WC; 18 Fire extinguisher CO_2 bottle; 19 Panel-type air filter; 20 (Side elevation) Fuel tank; 20 (Plan) Water filling ducts; 21 Cooker and No 2 equipment frame; 22 Header tank; 23 Emergency fuel tank; 24 Battery.

the engine coolant. The roof-mounted radiator fan was driven mechanically from the engine by an electro-magnetic coupling incorporated in the output side of the fan-drive right-angle gearbox. The clutch was a two-speed unit with thermo-electric control also operating the position of the shutters on the radiator air-inlet frames.

The main generator was an English Electric type 840/B unit with twelve compensated-poles, being of single bearing design with a continuous rating of 66kW, 600amp, 110V at 850rpm. The overhung auxiliary generator of type 911/5C was attached to this. Self-ventilation was used. Voltage output was controlled by a Newton Derby carbon-pile voltage regulator, all the auxiliaries being driven by this supply.

The six 538A traction motors were of four-pole type with dc series winding rated at 400hp, 533amp, 600V, and were axle-hung nose-suspended units with force ventilation. They were placed behind the axle for the leading pair and ahead for the trailing axle, and drove through a single reduction gear, ratio 53:18.

Roller-bearing suspension bearings were incorporated and the suspension arranged to minimise load transfer. Motors were electrically interconnected between bogies to give three series pairs in parallel across the generator. The power circuit gave full, two intermediate, and weak fields by field divert resistors.

The locomotive was completed at VF in spring 1962 and made its first trip on BR metals on 2 May 1962 when it ran light from Newton-le-Willows to Chester and back. Obviously the locomotive had been subjected to extensive tests

P2 at work on the LMR in 1962. *(GEC Traction Ltd)*

On its initial BR trials DP2 worked on the West Coast route of the LMR, and is here seen arriving at Rugby with an up express in 1962. *(GEC Traction Ltd)*

Following its first major overhaul after running over 360,000 miles on BR, and repainting in BR Deltic livery, DP2 returned to ER service and is here seen leaving Kings Cross with the down Sheffield Pullman on 3 August 1965. *(GEC Traction Ltd)*

at VF before this, but it only did one more test run before it was handed over to BR for revenue earning service.

The test was on 8 May, when it took a 15-coach train of 475 tons between Crewe and Penrith, 122 miles involving fast running. During the trip the train passed Tebay at 80mph, six miles after tackling Grayrigg bank with its six mile climb of 1 in 131 and 1 in 106, continuing to climb the 1 in 75 Shap bank to reach the summit four miles at 43mph.

On 11 May the locomotive was lent to the LMR for crew training and, following a few Crewe-Birmingham runs, was allocated to Camden shed from 14 May, taking on regular passenger workings between Euston and Liverpool on a diagram comprising: 07.45 (08.15 SO) Euston-Liverpool; 14.05 Liverpool-Euston; 19.15 SX Euston-Perth (as far as Crewe); 00.30 SX Crewe-Euston parcels. This six-day working gave a daily total of 388 miles, or 3800-4000 per week, Sundays being maintenance days. Loadings were of 12 to 16 coaches in the 400-500 tons tare range.

The 1962/3 winter timetable saw DP2 on Euston-Carlisle trains covering 3600-3800 miles per week with 420 tons down as far as Crewe and 290 tons between Crewe and Carlisle. It has been estimated that in one year on such a duty DP2 would have attained an annual mileage of approximately 135,000.

Between May 1962 and May 1963 DP2 worked a regular turn covering the 01.2. Euston-Carlisle and 13.25 Carlisle-Euston with maintenance on Sundays.

After completing about 130,000 miles on the above, DP2 moved to Euston-Blackpool job from 6 May 1963 working the 17.0. Euston-Blackpool and 08.00 Blackpool-Euston completing its week's work with the Sunda 07.45 Blackpool-Euston followed by maintenance until needed for Monday's 17.05 t Blackpool.

On this service loads varied from 486 ton Euston-Crewe, 410 tons Crewe-Preston, to 28 tons Preston-Blackpool, with similar retur loadings. This continued, giving a weekl mileage of about 2,800, until mid-June 1963.

So successful was DP2 that on the Blackpoc service the maker's engineer ceased to supervis the locomotive except on journeys immediatel before and after maintenance; it was thus left i the hands of BR crews and therefore unde normal service conditions comparable to othe BR diesel locomotives. The oft-levelled criticisn that prototypes were always specially treate could therefore no longer be levelled at DP2.

During its first 12 months DP2 covered ove

151,000 miles with absolute reliability. Its extra power certainly eased the task of making up lost time. In June 1963, after completing 164,580 miles, it was taken out of service for tyre turning at VF. In the 13 months up to 16 June DP2 had covered a total of 220,000 miles with only two on-line failures. One was in severe weather conditions in January 1963; when hauling the 01.31 Carlisle-Euston south of Crewe outside radiator panels froze due to prolonged slow running and a 30min signal stop, and caused the engine to shut-down with low water level. The other was a minor flashover, also south of Crewe, DP2 bringing its train into Crewe where it was taken off for examination. The locomotive picked up its return London working the same afternoon.

By 16 June engine hours stood at 4500, and while at VF for attention to its tyres the engine received its 5000hr inspection. Cylinder heads were taken off but the liners, piston rings, and big-end bearings were found in excellent condition, and the heads were replaced. Electrical equipment was cleaned and inspected, and a new train heating boiler of Clayton Mk II type was fitted.

On the LMR DP2 had worked the heaviest and fastest trains, but the schedules were based on those of the Class 40 2000bhp diesels, allowing little opportunity for full capacity working. To correct this, the English Electric Co made arrangements for it to run on the ER East Coast route, so that it would be subjected to long periods of hard work among the most intensive passenger schedules on BR, where the 22 English Electric Deltic locomotives of 3300bhp were doing up to 200,000 miles annually.

DP2 was moved to the ER at Finsbury Park depot in July 1963, and was found to have arrived at an opportune time, for the Deltics were being taken out of traffic one by one to enable boiler modifications to be undertaken. DP2 was thus put into the Deltic pool and allocated their diagrams, no mean feat for a 2700bhp unit. On 13 July it worked from Kings Cross to Leeds and back, but from 15 July it was given Kings Cross diagram 7, comprising:

Sunday: Maintenance
              17.10   Kings Cross-Newcastle

Monday: 00.46   Newcastle-Kings Cross
              10.10   Kings Cross-Edinburgh
              22.30   Edinburgh-Kings Cross

Tuesday to Friday, inclusive:
              10.10   Kings Cross-Edinburgh
              22.30   Edinburgh-Kings Cross

Saturday: 10.10   Kings Cross-Edinburgh
              20.05   Edinburgh-Kings Cross

DP2 thus had a weekly mileage of 5,270 in its seven day diagram, including 115 hours of running, six return trips to Edinburgh, and one to Newcastle. Maintenance was carried out on Sundays between 08.30 and 15.30. Although it was thought more time would be needed for monthly and three-monthly examinations, this proved not to be the case because of the trouble-free running and ease of maintenance.

The 10.10 Kings Cross-Edinburgh was usually loaded to 13 coaches, weighing 440 tons tare, and called at Newcastle only, for 3min and to change crews, arriving at Edinburgh at 16.30. The train had an average of 62.5mph, and experience showed that under normal driving conditions DP2 could gain up to 10min on the 4hr 17min schedule to Newcastle. On the route north of Newcastle speed restrictions usually prevented further time-gaining. The return working, 22.30 from Edinburgh, usually had 14 coaches, taring at 450 tons and was given just under seven hours for the run to Kings Cross.

By early September DP2 had covered over 200,000 miles, so that by the end of the summer timetable it was withdrawn and sent to Robert Stephenson and Hawthorns Ltd at Darlington for new bogies of modified type, but similar to those of the Class 37 units of BR.

On the basis that DP2 had run for 58 consecutive days, covering 43,000 trouble-free miles on the East Coast route, a yearly mileage

TABLE 20
MAIN DETAILS AND DIMENSIONS OF PROTOTYPE LOCOMOTIVE DP2

Description	*Data*
Axle layout	Co-Co
Engine model	16CSVT
Engine rating	2700BHP at 850rpm
Locomotive weight, in working order	105 tons 0cwt
Locomotive weight, empty	97 tons 2cwt
Brakes, locomotive	Straight air
Brakes, train	Air continuous vacuum
Train heating	Clayton R02500 boiler
Boiler water supply	640 gals
Length over buffers	69ft 6in
Overall width	8ft 9½in
Overall height	12ft 10in
Wheel diameter	3ft 7in
Bogie pivots	45ft 0in
Bogie wheelbase	13ft 6in
Total wheelbase	58ft 6in
Maximum speed	90mph
Maximum tractive effort	50,000 lb
Continuous tractive effort	35,500 lb at 23.3mph
Locomotive and boiler fuel capacity	900gals

The end of a remarkable locomotive. DP2 was badly damaged after colliding with a derailed cement train on an adjacent track near Thirsk on 31 July 1967. *(John M. Boyes)*

of around 250,000 miles would have been obtained.

DP2 had its first major overhaul in mid-1965, after running 360,000 miles in revenue earning service since 1962, re-entering ER service on 3 August with the 11.20 Sheffield Pullman, adorned in its new Deltic style two-tone green livery, much more attractive than its sombre plain green original guise.

During the spring of 1966 DP2 was fitted with a new control system incorporating electronic tractive effort and wheel-slip control. On its trials the locomotive took a 16 coach test train from the Vulcan Works to Penrith with a stop and restart at Scout Green Box on Shap Bank. With the aid of its new equipment, DP2 restarted the train to attain 30mph within a few hundred yards. An already excellent locomotive was improved by its new equipment, and it was evidently capable of out-accelerating a Deltic locomotive up to 20mph.

Back on the ER, some spirited running was made with Kings Cross-Cambridge trains, far superior to anything achieved previously. Early 1966 saw it on Kings Cross-Leeds services. In the summer DP2 was on London-Edinburgh duties, such as the Anglo-Scottish Car-Carrier which ran between Holloway and Perth, frequently, being on this train until the end of the summer service in September. It was on this train that

DP2 was derailed outside Waverley Station, Edinburgh on 4 August, resulting in its absence until the 30th.

During October/November DP2 spent some time on Kings Cross-Cambridge trains as filling in turns for its workings on the 01.15 Kings Cross-York and 08.00 York-Kings Cross. It continued thus into January 1967, when it put in some appearance on the White Rose between Kings Cross and Leeds, before returning to Anglo-Scottish workings.

The derailment of the 02.50 Cliffe-Uddingston cement train running on the down goods line near Thirsk on 31 July 1967 was most unfortunate; DP2 running at speed on the adjoining down fast line with an express could not stop before hitting the cement wagons across its path. DP2 sustained severe front and left hand side damage, and was taken to York shed where it lay sheeted over until September, when it was moved to the Vulcan works of English Electric. No real progress was made on repair work and the locomotive was dismantled in 1968.

The demise of DP2 in this way was indeed a tragedy, for probably this locomotive was the most successful prototype diesel-electric ever built, having run over 600,000 miles on BR. DP2 carried Vulcan works number D733 and English Electric 3205 of 1961.

CHAPTER 12

D400 CLASS

Following the undoubted success of the English Electric prototype DP2, BR ordered a batch of 2700bhp Co-Co diesel-electrics, in co-operation with English Electric, for use on the West Coast route of the LMR. They were to act as a stop-gap prior to the completion of electrification between Euston and Glasgow, but intended to work chiefly north of Crewe.

The contract was negotiated to give work continuity to the locomotive mechanical portion section of Vulcan Foundry and at the same time provide BR with a high-power high-speed locomotive capable of sustained rated engine output not attainable with their own standard 2750bhp units.

The question as to why higher-powered locomotives were not obtained seems to be answered by the intention to transfer the locomotives to the WR to replace their last diesel-hydraulic locomotives, higher power units being thought more difficult to re-employ.

It was anticipated that an order for fifty DP2 type locomotives would simply result in a production batch of the prototype but, while this might have been the hope of English Electric, BR had other ideas when the order was placed in 1966. By now BR had decreed that a flat front body design was imperative, so DP2 with its Deltic outline was a non-starter in this respect, while other directives from BR were to turn a bread and butter locomotive into a most sophisticated and internally-cramped locomotive with nevertheless revolutionary characteristics.

Vulcan Foundry drawing office produced an attractive front-end design with wrap-round triplex windscreen, but this was lost due to BR requirements for cab layout. In this rethink the cab front lower-panel mounted train indicator box and provision for jumper cables was lost for the ugly roof-mounted box and cab front clutter we see today.

Construction started at Vulcan works in early 1967, the plan being not to sell these locomotives to BR, but lease-hire them. A special company was formed named English Electric Leasings Ltd and a small oval plate midway along the bodyside stated 'This locomotive is the property of English Electric Leasings Ltd.' Numbered D400-49, they were soon given BR diesel

classification 50 and in 1973/4 renumbered in the 50001-50 series.

The D400 locomotives were indeed a milestone in British diesel traction, being fitted with the same basic engine as that installed 20 years before in 10000/1, but virtually doubling in power to weight ratio, giving 70 per cent more power per cylinder. The D400s it was hoped, combined in one locomotive the possibility of greatly increased power output per ton of weight, a high standard of reliability for all types of duties, and maximum equipment efficiency. The advanced technology applied to these locomotives gave automatic tractive effort control, dynamic braking, inertia filtration, and slow-speed control.

Solid state devices were used in the D400 power-control equipment, particularly in the control of the main generator current output. This stemmed from English Electric work in thyristors in electric multiple-unit sets. The D400s were the world's first high-power diesel electrics so equipped.

It was felt that as the performance of a diesel-electric locomotive is extended in range by employing field-weakening in the traction motors as acceleration builds up, it was important to control this accurately by using an electronic time delay unit in the appropriate control circuits, and thus give a simple precise control of the field weakening switches.

The main generator current is regulated by a closed loop control system which receives input signals from the driver's controller, the diesel engine governor, current in the traction motor circuits, and the speedometer. The outputs from these sources are fed via operational amplifiers which control the KV10 chopper circuit supplying the main generator field. This control system regulates the tractive effort, diesel engine load, and the speed of the train in response to signals from the driver, which it compares with the signals proportional to the tractive effort required.

An output signal is then provided, which operates the thyristor controller for the main generator field so that the locomotive performs as calculated. The system is able to correct any wheelslip troubles automatically, so that if,

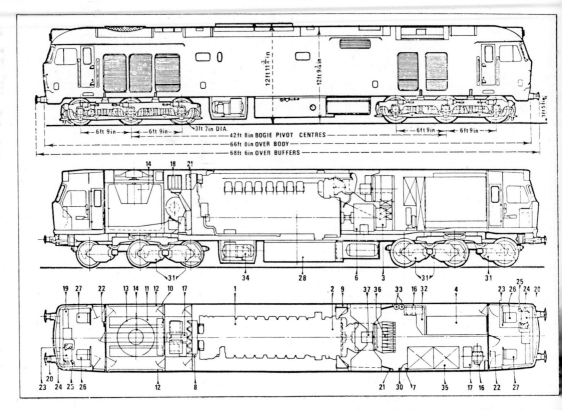

Fig 15: Layout of English Electric 2700bhp Co-Co diesel electric of BR class 50, developed to BR requirements following the success of DP2. Key: 1 Engine 16 CSVT; 2 Main generator EE 840; 3 Auxiliary generator E 911; 4 Main equipment frame; 5 Batteries; 6 Train heating generator; 7 Urinal; 8 Engine fuel supply unit; 9 Engine air ducting; 10 Radiator header tank; 11 Radiators; 12 Radiator shutters; 13 Radiator fan; 14 Radiator fan motor; 15 Compressor WTG 3VC75; 16 Exhausters; 17 Traction motor blowers; 18 Air filters; 19 Sand fillers; 20 Driver's desk; 21 Air filters; 22 Handbrake; 23 Master controller; 24 Automatic air brake valve; 25 Independent air brake valve; 26 Driver's seat; 27 Assistant's seat; 28 Main 1,000gal fuel tank; 29 Main fuel tank gauge; 30 Urinal flush tank; 31 Traction motors EE 538; 32 Brake equipment; 33 CO$_2$ bottles; 34 Air reservoirs; 35 Dynamic brake; 36 Air filter (equipment compartment); 37 Fan motor. *(Author's collection)*

when working, the adhesive weight will not sustain the tractive effort chosen by the driver, the automatic tractive effort control imposes a lower one, giving a great advantage when starting heavy loads. A Westinghouse anti-slip brake is also installed.

The driver of a D400 has the advantage of being able to preset the tractive effort he requires, this being maintained constantly throughout acceleration. This gives the class the ability to perform more consistently no matter what conditions they operate under, and also more efficiently uses the electrical equipment. The whole of the control equipment is housed in a single cubicle. The use of dynamic-braking, of the electro-mechanical type, improved braking efficiency, minimising brake rigging and block wear, both systems being integrated automatically and controlled by the driver with one handle.

Inertia filtration, specified by BR, comprising primary and secondary disposable dry-pack elements, replaced the usual oil-wetted air filters. One primary system provides air to No 1 end traction motor blower and, via a secondary system, to the two No 1 end engine turbo-blowers. No 2 end was similar, with the primary supplying the traction motor blower, the main generator, and dynamic brake compartment and the remaining two turbo-blowers. Dirt extraction is by a motor-driven fan.

The requirement for slow-speed operation needed by BR for merry-go-round train working where speeds below 3mph are necessary, is provided for by a driver-operated pre-set speed control system, automatically maintained without variation, regardless of trailing load or gradient. An electronic speedometer linked to the electronic control system is fitted which, at a given speed, will signal and initiate automatic control for slow-speed-working.

Equipment for push-pull working was installed, and up to three D400s could operate in multiple, but although initially only D400/1 had the jumper cables fitted, all locomotives were wired internally.

The engine is the English Electric 16 cylinder 16 CSVT turbo-charged and charge air-cooled engine giving 2700bhp at 850rpm, identical to that operated so successfully in DP2. The radiator fan speed is automatically varied by an electronic sensing device to match cooling requirements, and obviates power wastage in driving a fan at a rate which may not be necessary, while at the same time keeping the engine at the most efficient working temperature. Spiral tube radiators in pairs of panels are mounted one behind the other on each side of the locomotive. The outer panels are interconnected to cool the charge-air coolers and lubricating oil cooler. The inner panels cool the engine cooling water and turbo-blower water. The main generator is the English Electric model 840/4B machine, rated continuously at 1800amp, 970V at 850rpm. The auxiliary generator, an EE 911/5C unit, is, as in normal EE practice, overhung from the free end of the train-heating generator. Its output is constant at 110V, being kept so by a static voltage regulator. Excitation of the main generator is through a KV10 field supply unit.

The D400 class is the first high power diesel-electric to be built for BR equipped from new for electric train heating. An EE 915/1B train-heating generator, driven by a cardan shaft from the main generator, is rated continuously at 32kW at 850rpm and giving 800V dc down to 550rpm, and 650V at 450rpm idling speed. The output voltage is constantly maintained by the KV10 field supply unit in conjunction with a NPE 7 control unit.

The six English Electric axle-hung nose-suspended traction motors are of type EE 538/5A, similar to those of the BR D6700 and Deltic locomotives. SKF and Timken axle roller suspension are provided, with oil-seals to prevent ingress of gear lubricant to the suspension bearings. Suspension tubes, electrically insulated from the axle, are provided, while the motors on each bogie are interconnected by earthing cables connected to the bogie frame, which in turn is earthed to the locomotive body. The traction motors are connected in series-parallel without equaliser connections, three stages of field weakening being provided.

The mechanical portion is conventional, being based on two full length rolled steel joists, tied by fabricated cross-members forming the underframe. The top is plated and sealed with oil drains provided, leading into a collecting tank. The bogies are standard with those of the

A general view of the first of the class, D400, as built. (GEC Traction Ltd)

D6700 and Deltic classes, but modified to enable the installation of weight-transfer compensation equipment if ever needed. D417 was in fact fitted with this equipment, but so sure footed were these locomotives that it proved to be no advantage and it was subsequently removed.

Standard Timken roller bearing axleboxes are used and the wheel tyres have the modified Heumann profile. The interior of the driving cab is to the BR Design Panel layout with heat/sound insulation and forced-air ventilation; an electronic device switches off all lights, except tail lights, 15min after stopping the engine. The class is fitted with the standard four-digit indicator box mounted on the front of the cab roof canopy.

By early May 1967 construction of the order at Vulcan Foundry had reached the stage of engine installation in the first two examples, but the first deliveries into running stock at Crewe depot did not occur until October with D400, painted rail blue with full yellow front.

The section north of Crewe, to Glasgow, was to be the almost exclusive haunt of the D400 class. This hilly route presented some difficulty to diesel traction and was notably more difficult than the Crewe-Euston section operated by electric traction. The D400s were expected to run their part of the run to Glasgow at speeds not noticeably less than those achieved by electric traction south of Crewe. Complete

deliveries took 12 months, all 50 locomotives being allocated to Crewe depot.

D400/1 fitted for multiple operation from new, complete with jumper cables, were put to use immediately on driver training, to be followed on this task by D402/4—lent to Polmadie depot in Scotland. D406 was sent to the Research Centre at Derby in early 1968, to be joined by D401 in April, D406 not being taken into stock until April 1968.

Their introduction on West Coast services was gradual, but it involved the complete replacement on all main diagrams of other Type 4 diesels, the Mid-Day Scot being in their hands, together with some Birmingham-Glasgow trains by early 1968. Although not fitted for, nor intended for, Glasgow-Edinburgh push-pull services, D405 was on 100mph trials on this route in April 1968.

By May about two dozen were at work, taking by then most passenger and Freightliner work, and being frequently seen at Glasgow, Perth, and Edinburgh. In June they took on Glasgow-Liverpool services, while the same month's labour dispute caused them to be seen on diverted trains over the Waverley route to and from Glasgow on Glasgow-Perth and Euston trains.

By mid-summer a dramatic change had overtaken the West Coast services, with the D400 class on all main workings and effectively demoting all their predecessors. This meant that

The down Midland Scot at Beattock Summit with two class 50s, Nos D445 and D412, in multiple on 1 August 1970. *(Derek Cross)*

all trains from Euston and Glasgow, north of Crewe, together with Birmingham, Liverpool, and Manchester-Glasgow were D400 hauled.

By September 1968 construction at Vulcan Works had reached 442-9. Proposals to operate the class in multiple on Anglo-Scottish duties, as envisaged by the fitting of D400/1, were tried out in late 1968, when D405 and D418 were tested on the up Mid-Day Scot from Glasgow. The potential of this combination gave the Crewe-Scotland services a high-speed capability never before possible. The lack of high-power diesels on the LMR and the difficulty in maintaining similar high speed schedules to those of the East Coast route, with its fleet of 3300bhp Deltic locomotives, was one which caused many to wonder why the LMR had not obtained similar locomotives.

This apparent return to the old small-engine policy reminiscent of the 1920s and early 1930s, with a preponderence of 2000/2500bhp units not capable of being stretched to meet growing airline competition has never been satisfactorily explained, although impending electrification provided a good excuse that too many high-power diesels would prove difficult to redeploy elsewhere. Another theory was that the heavy overnight traffic on the West Coast route demanded more locomotives than during day time, thus permitting multiple operation to provide power for accelerated services while at the same time making full use of motive power.

The capabilities of the D400 class were soon apparent. A run with D416 in April 1969 on the 16.15 Glasgow-Euston, composed of nine coaches with a 34min late departure from Carlisle, saw time gained all the way to Preston. The train passed Penrith, 17½ miles, in 17min, Shap Summit in 30min, to pass Carnforth in 57¼min despite a severe check at Tebay and a slowing near Hincaster. By Preston 17min had been gained, giving a net running time of 78½min for the 90 miles, an average speed of almost 70mph.

Visits of the class to the East Coast at Newcastle were not unknown, but in spring 1969 at least three, D405/8/9, visited Darlington for bogie rotational tests at the Bank Top turntable. Plans for the 1970/1 timetable, to commence on

4 May, involved faster and more regular Anglo-Scottish trains with new rolling stock, cutting up to 45min from journey times. Euston-Glasgow was given up to 65min saving in the up direction, and 55min down, while 50min was lopped off the fastest Liverpool, Manchester-Glasgow timings. To meet these requirements Crewe works was busy fitting the D400s with jumper cables for multiple operation.

D400s in multiple became more common as spring approached, and it was during this period of pairing that the relatively low availability became noticeable, for their use in multiple effectively reduced the class by half. So with at times only 60 per cent available for traffic the approach of the new timetable was no doubt viewed with some trepidation.

It is perhaps pertinent at this point to survey some of the problems which beset the class, and indeed started early. English Electric guaranteed an availability of 84 per cent for the D400s, and EE engineers were based at the depots at which the locomotives were likely to be stopped— Crewe, Carlisle and Polmadie. If a locomotive was stopped due to either party, BR or EE, an appropriate penalty was paid. Engine troubles began by bent connecting rods splitting the cylinder liner and causing water dilution of the engine lubricating oil. This proved difficult to resolve and affected engines of two to three months old. It was finally traced to a crack in the cylinder head waterways allowing cooling water to enter the cylinder and cause a hydraulic action, especially after the engines had cooled following standing. New cylinder heads, at first Mark II, and then Mark III were fitted at weekends at both Vulcan Works and Crewe works.

Engine power output was liable to fluctuate downwards when the hydraulic-type engine governor, with its inbuilt power protection unit, reacted to conditions of low air charge and cut down the fuel flow to the engine. This device in practice often prevented the engine from developing its full power when the charge air was all right!

Failure of the little ends severely damaged some engines and in combination with the splitting of the cylinder liners, caused some engines to be written-off. The result was that there were only 48 engines for 50 locomotives, although availability of the engine from DP2, initially in D400 which had been out of traffic for some months following a runaway accident at Beattock, eased the situation. To this day there are fewer engines than locomotives with the result that at least one locomotive remains in works awaiting the next overhauled engine. The little end problem was traced to lack of oil due to a too severe piston scraper ring. Removal of the ring resulted in a massive increase in lubricating oil consumption and at engine idling speeds, oil was to be seen pouring out of the exhausts. A less severe scraper ring was later refitted. The seizing up of the turbo-chargers has been a recurring problem but water leaks at pipe connections from manifold to turbo-charger were cured by modified pipelines.

Some difficulties with train heating generators and voltage variations between 600-1000V caused shut downs at high voltage to protect the generator. Initially engines were set to idle faster to reduce the range to 800-1000V. Later the rolling stock was found to have earthing troubles and the problem was solved.

Once the new timetable came into operation the following trains were diagrammed for paired D400 haulage:

Glasgow-Euston: 07.40, 10.00 (The Royal Scot), 12.00, 14.00, 16.00.
Glasgow and Edinburgh-Birmingham: 17.30 (The Midland Scot).
Glasgow-Manchester and Liverpool: 18.00.
Liverpool and Manchester-Glasgow: 08.15.
Birmingham-Glasgow: 08.15 (The Midland Scot).
Euston-Glasgow: 08.00, 10.05 (The Royal Scot), 12.05, 14.05, 16.05.

The use of D400s in multiple gave a combined output of 5400bhp, or about 4140 at rail, allowing for power taken by auxiliaries, train-heating, etc; on the steep gradients of Shap and Beattock such power was very necessary for 12 coach, 430 gross tons loads, and to give the acceleration required for recovering from permanent way and signal hold-ups and from station stops. The locomotives had, in fact, a more difficult task than the electric locomotives south of Crewe. D400 class locomotives were also firmly established on fast freight and Freightliner trains, being seen frequently on the Settle-Carlisle line, in addition to the West Coast route.

The first day of the accelerations saw some good performances. One, with 409 and 430 on the 14.05 Euston-Glasgow, loaded to 12 vehicles of 425 tons gross, left Crewe and encountered delays at Hartford and Weaver Junction, resulting in some fast running to reach 100/101mph near Balshaw Lane. Preston, 52

Class 50 No 50040 on the northbound Winsford-Tyne Yard salt train nears Armathwaite on the Settle & Carlisle line on 23 June 1975. *(Brian Webb)*

miles from Crewe, was passed in 49min, 101/102mph being reached near Garstang; Lancaster was passed at 66mph, with a net time of 16½min from Preston. Carnforth and Milnthorpe again saw speeds of 101/102mph. On the 13 miles 1 in 100/1 in 50 of Grayrigg Bank, a steady 75mph was maintained and Tebay passed at 96mph. Shap Summit was topped at 73mph, progress being impeded by a 10mph restriction at Penrith, although 97/98mph was reached between there and Carlisle.

At the end of 1971 the availability of the D400 locomotives, or Class 50, as they were now officially termed, in relation to other English Electric diesel-electrics of BR, was:

Class	Number in Service	Availability (Per Cent)	Average Miles Run per Year	Average Miles Run per Casualty
55 Deltic	22	75	144,000	14,000
50 D400	50	70	103,000	9,000
40 D200	199	80	57,000	13,000
37 D6700	308	88	52,000	40,000

Although from these figures the Class 50 came out worst, reports from technical staff are such as to indicate much higher actual mileages of around 150,000 per year, or twice that for the competitive 2750bhp locomotives operating on the LMR. It must be remembered, though, that the Class 50s were on high mileage high-speed diagrams. The figures of around 150,000 miles are supported by the amount of running gear maintenance necessary, as difficulty was experienced with the Class 50s which had similar engine hours to the competitive locomotives but double the mileage. Brake blocks flanging round the wheels caused thermal cracks and loose tyres, and modified blocks did not alleviate the problem. Further modifications with rubbing plates is in hand for these locomotives and the Deltics which have the same bogie. Attempts to get more main works attention for the bogies was difficult but replacement of running gear with reconditioned sets proved a great advance.

In 1972 it was revealed that the Class 50 costs only 9p per mile to operate, while the Deltics cost 27p and the 2700bhp WR diesel-hydraulics

24p at 75 per cent availability. So just how does one measure the success or otherwise of a locomotive?

A typical 1972 exploit of paired Class 50s was with the 14.00 Glasgow-Euston with 12 coaches of 420 tons gross. With 100min allowed for the 102.90 miles to Carlisle they often completed it in 90min with speed continuously over 75mph, and mostly in the top 80/lower 90 bracket; maxima of 101-103 were frequently reached between Beattock and Carlisle. Later that year the author timed a similar load from Crewe to Carlisle in 126min on the 131min schedule for the 141 miles.

On this run speeds of 105/6mph were recorded twice, first about five miles south of Warrington, following permanent way slacks and speed restrictions near Winsford, and after this point so that Warrington was passed 2min late. Lancaster, 71.95 miles from Crewe, was passed in 77min on a 65min schedule so that time had to be made up. Time recovery started at Oxenholme, speeds from thence to Tebay not falling below 85mph, Tebay being passed at 96mph, and Shap Fell climbed at not less than 70mph. The maximum of the run was achieved near Southwaite with 106mph, so that Carlisle was reached 5min inside schedule. Such speeds and higher—110 being reported by train crews—were common once the new schedules were established. The miners' strike of early 1972 brought the class more regularly into London when they deputised for electric traction.

The planned replacement of the WR 2700bhp Class 52 diesel-hydraulics by the 50s upon completion of the West Coast electrification to Glasgow was indicated by the move of D400 to Bristol Bath Road depot on 11 October 1972, being soon joined by D401. They spent a long time on training work with odd forays as necessary, D400 itself breaking new ground with the 15.58 Bristol-Plymouth parcels in June 1973 by making the first trip of the type over the South Devon banks. D401 worked the 15.15 Bristol-Paddington on 24 June.

The continued partisanship of the WR enthusiasts saw to it that every failing of these

TABLE 21
MAIN DETAILS AND DIMENSIONS OF D400 CLASS, LATER CLASS 50

Description	*Data*
Axle layout	Co-Co
Engine model	16CSVT
Engine rating	2700BHP at 850rpm
Locomotive weight, in working order	115 tons 1cwt
Locomotive weight, empty	111 tons 3cwt
Brakes, locomotive	Straight air/automatic air
Brakes, train	Automatic air/air continuous vacuum
Train heating	Electric generator driven from main generator
Length over buffers	68ft 6in
Overall width	9ft 1¼in
Overall height	12ft 11 3/4in
Wheel diameter	3ft 7in
Bogie pivots	42ft 8in
Bogie wheelbase	13ft 6in
Total wheelbase	56ft 2in
Maximum speed	100mph
Maximum tractive effort	48,500 lb at 18.8% adhesion
Continuous tractive effort	33,000 lb at 23.5mph
Continuous rail hp	2070
Locomotive fuel capacity	1055gals

sophisticated and unfamiliar locomotives was fully covered in the press, while the diesel-hydraulic fleet, which by their uniqueness fitted in nicely to the old GWR spirit to go it alone, continued to be upheld by their protagonists as the masters, in spite of their high maintenance costs, and the lack of main works repair facilities.

With the extension of electrification between Crewe and Preston from 23 July 1973, the change-over point from electric to diesel traction became Preston for most Anglo-Scottish trains. The Royal Scot, however, continued to change locomotives at Crewe. On 26 July, 429 and 441 with the down Royal Scot completed the Euston-Glasgow run in 5 hours 43min, the Carlisle-Glasgow section being run at an average of 78.8mph in spite of a series of permanent way slacks, regaining 1½min on schedule.

By this time, 400/1 on the WR were working a variety of Bristol duties ranging from Yeovil parcels trains, to Paddington expresses from Bristol and Weston-super-Mare.

A run recorded in late 1973 on the LMR during Sunday diversions because of electrification work on the main line, saw 408 and 407 take the 11.55 Glasgow-Euston over the Carlisle-Hellifield section of the Midland route. Loaded to 11 coaches, grossing 405 tons, the train left Carlisle 5½min down, but sped away to reach Cumwhinton at 75mph, the 4 miles having taken 6min 33sec. After a signal check near Low House, speed rose to 82mph by Lazonby, 15 miles, passing there in 17 min 27sec, the climb of 1 in 220 from Armathwaite through Barons Wood tunnels being taken at 76mph. Appleby, 30.75 miles, was passed at 78mph in 31min, good considering the route's 80mph limit. A peak of 91mph was reached briefly at Ormside viaduct. Ais Gill Box, 48.35 miles, was passed in 46min 8sec at 76mph, Garsdale at 73mph in 48min 37sec, Settle, 71.50 miles, in 67min 54sec, Hellifield being reached in 85min 45sec for the 76.7 miles from Carlisle.

The WR received its third example in January 1974 when 404 arrived at Bristol, being followed by 411 the following month. During December/January 1973/4 401 was at Old Oak Common for crew training, as it was now anticipated that casual electric workings on the LMR to Glasgow before full electric operation in May would release further D400s to the WR.

In March 1974 403/5/27 went to Bristol and then on to Plymouth Laira, the stronghold of the last WR diesel-hydraulics. The swan-song of the

LMR locomotives saw them putting in remarkable running, typified by 420 and 439 on the 08.00 Euston-Glasgow on 14 February. This train left Carlisle 23min late, but regained 10½min by Beattock, climbing the 10 mile bank in 7¾min and regaining 17min by Carstairs. In spite of checks on the run thence to Glasgow, the train still had a 4¾min gain when it drew into Glasgow Central.

Timekeeping remained good and trains consistently ran early even with only one locomotive, such as 445 on the 09.00 ex-Euston,

TABLE 22 D400 CLASS TYPE 4 – LATER BR CLASS 50

Original BR No	Works No Vulcan Wks	Works No Eng Elec	Date to Traffic	Reg New	Allo-cation Sep '75
D400	D1141	3770	P10/67	LM	W
D401	D1143	3772	P13/67	LM	W
D402	D1142	3771	P13/67	LM	W
D403	D1144	3773	P1/68	LM	W
D404	D1145	3774	P13/67	LM	W
D405	D1146	3775	P1/68	LM	W
D406	D1147	3776	P4/68	LM	LM
D407	D1148	3777	P3/68	LM	W
D408	D1149	3778	P3/68	LM	LM
D409	D1150	3779	P3/68	LM	W
D410	D1151	3780	P3/68	LM	LM
D411	D1152	3781	P3/68	LM	W
D412	D1153	3782	P3/68	LM	LM
D413	D1154	3783	P3/68	LM	W
D414	D1155	3784	P5/68	LM	W
D415	D1156	3785	P4/68	LM	W
D416	D1157	3786	P5/68	LM	W
D417	D1158	3787	P4/68	LM	LM
D418	D1159	3788	P4/68	LM	W
D419	D1160	3789	P5/68	LM	W
D420	D1161	3790	P5/68	LM	W
D421	D1162	3791	P5/68	LM	W
D422	D1163	3792	P5/68	LM	LM
D423	D1164	3793	P5/68	LM	W
D424	D1165	3794	P6/68	LM	W
D425	D1166	3795	P6/68	LM	W
D426	D1167	3796	P7/68	LM	W
D427	D1168	3797	P6/68	LM	W
D428	D1169	3798	P7/68	LM	W
D429	D1170	3799	P7/68	LM	LM
D430	D1171	3800	P7/68	LM	W
D431	D1172	3801	P7/68	LM	LM
D432	D1173	3802	P7/68	LM	W
D433	D1174	3803	P8/68	LM	W
D434	D1175	3804	P8/68	LM	LM
D435	D1176	3805	P8/68	LM	LM
D436	D1177	3806	P9/68	LM	LM
437	D1178	3807	P10/68	LM	W
438	D1179	3808	P10/68	LM	W
439	D1180	3809	P10/68	LM	W
440	D1181	3810	P10/68	LM	LM
441	D1182	3811	P10/68	LM	LM
442	D1183	3812	P10/68	LM	W
443	D1184	3813	P10/68	LM	W
444	D1185	3814	P11/68	LM	W
445	D1186	3815	P11/68	LM	LM
446	D1187	3816	P11/68	LM	W
447	D1188	3817	P12/68	LM	W
448	D1189	3818	P12/68	LM	W
449	D1190	3819	P13/68	LM	W

which was 14½min early into Carlisle, while renumbered locomotives 50040 and 50031 on the down Royal Scot were 20min early into the Border City on 2 March 1974.

Electric working to Glasgow permitted 31 more Class 50s to be moved to the WR during April/May, leaving the LMR with only 12, later increased to 15 by the return of three from the WR. The LMR retained these for use on the G & SWR route to Glasgow via Kilmarnock, which was not electrified, although they are used on a variety of duties, such as diverted trains due to maintenance on electrified routes, via the Carlisle-Settle line. Their use on parcels, freights, and Freightliner trains is common, while their visits to the Tyneside area on freights has become more common. The retention of these locomotives by the LMR showed that there was still reluctance to rely on other Type 4 diesels for principal passenger services when running off the electrified lines for any reason.

Although the WR was slow to adjust to its new acquisitions, the capability of the D400s was soon proved by loads of up to 400 tons on Bristol/South Wales-Paddington services with speeds in the 80-100mph range, thereby exceeding the Western class diesel-hydraulics, with their lower maximum speed of 90mph.

As WR crews gained expertise on the more complex controls of the D400s they soon realised their speed potential, and for the first time ever WR passengers on some routes were able to enjoy regular running at, or over, 100mph, diesel-electric traction giving the Western Region this new speed dimension. Up to 15 Class 50 units could soon be seen daily at Paddington, and the number increased gradually.

A multiple working with 50007 and 50046 in July saw them take the 22.15 Paddington-Bristol to arrive at Swindon so early as to have to stand 16½min before continuing to Bristol. On the WR the Class 50 has not reached the brilliance of the LMR West Coast but WR timings, loads and gradients did not demand such a high level of performance.

From the end of 1974 the LMR members of the class were used for some months to haul diverted LMR West Coast route trains over the Settle & Carlisle route to permit reballasting of the track on the electrified main line on Sundays. The first months of 1975 saw some of the LMR examples working in multiple on services to Inverness, while May saw the move of 50021 to the WR depleting the LMR fleet to 14

locomotives though without altering their workings; as a result it was still possible to see them on the LMR in the London, Crewe, Preston, and Carlisle areas, with prolific appearances on Settle & Carlisle line freights.

As the WR diesel-hydraulic fleet declined further the Western will need to augment its 2700/2750bhp diesel-electric stock, and it would seem logical for the WR to take the remaining LMR Class 50s in due course, unless train service cuts, discussed as this book went to press, reduce the WR's motive power requirements.

The Class 50 may be regarded as the final development of the true BR high-speed mixed-traffic diesel-electric locomotive, for future thinking for passenger trains centres on the multiple-unit concept found in the High Speed Train and Advanced Passenger Train. A logical bread and butter derivative of the Class 50 was the 1969 batch of ten EE 2700bhp units for service in Portugal. They are the most powerful UK diesel-electric locomotives yet exported to a specific overseas order and have put in some excellent work alongside a much larger fleet of 1350bhp English Electric diesels derived from the BR Class 20.

TABLE 23
RECLASSIFICATION AND RENUMBERING OF
ENGLISH ELECTRIC LINE SERVICE
DIESEL-ELECTRICS ON BR

Power Type Class	New Class	Original Number Series	Details of Renumbering	
4	40	D200-399	D200	40122
			D201-321	40001-121
			D322	scrapped
			D323-99	40123-199
4	50	D400-49	D400	50050
			D401-49	50001-49
2	23	D5900-09	withdrawn before renumbering	
3	37	D6700-999	D6700	37119
		D6600-08	D6701-818	37001-118
			D6819	37283
			D6820-6982	37120-282
			D6983	scrapped
			D6984-99 & D6600-08	37284-37308
1	20	D8000-199	D8000	20050
		D8300-27	D8001-49	20001-49
			D8050	20128
			D8051-127	20051-127
			D8128	20228
			D8129-99 & D8300-27	20129-227
5	55	D9000-21	D9000	55022
			D9001-21	55001-21

INDEX